Be Strong and Brave

How a child's faith saved his life

NICOLE PIERSON

Printed in the United States of America
Cover design by Dylan Geist
Edited by Michelle Krueger, SW Content

Pierson, Nicole.
    Be Strong and Brave: How a child's faith saved his
life / Nicole Pierson. -First edition
        pages cm
ISBN-13: 978-0692672860 (paperback) 1. Faith 2. Miracles 3.
Inspirational 4. Pierson, Gavin, 2006-   I. Title.

Dedicated To

My son, full of hope and faith. Gavin, you never stopped being strong and brave. Through pain and suffering, you continued to believe that you would make it and because of your will and faith, we all fought harder. I am so very proud to be your mother.

Prologue

Dreams give us an escape from reality. Sometimes they are terrifying and we wake up grateful they are not true. As my eyes finally close with dried tears on my cheeks, I drift away to what our life was supposed to be.

The waves are crashing wildly against the shore in a beautiful, predictable pattern. My feet are buried deep in the white sand as I close my eyes and listen to the sounds that encompass my being in perfect harmony. The weight of the sand brings a sense of being grounded, still and at peace. I peel one eye open, one hand over my face to shade the sun, and look at Steve next to me. We created this. We have control. This is the life we imagined. I dig my heels deeper trying to stay.

The sunlight dances across Gavin's and Gage's cheeks as they build a sandcastle a few feet away, close enough to be protected. Their sun-kissed, blonde hair complements the blue sky surrounding them. My children are untouched by the cruelty of this world, they are free from hospitals and pain. My breaths are steady and calm as I watch Grace doing cartwheels excitedly, "Mom, I just did four in a row and I didn't even stop!" she shouts. I smile at her never-ending determination and need for adventure.

In this blissful moment, I am overwhelmed with peace. Everything is as it should be. As I close my eyes once again, soaking it all in, there's a beeping in the background that is overshadowing the calming sound of the waves. My breaths begin to match its sudden, alarming pattern. I try to focus in on everything one more time, knowing I must leave this place. It is fading away quickly though, and there is nothing I can do to stop it.

When I was a child, I vividly remember dreaming that I finally got the cabbage patch doll I had wanted so badly. I realized, while still dreaming, that I would have to wake up at some point and my newly acquired doll would be gone. I held the doll extra tight, hoping somehow I would be able to take her with me. When I woke up, she was gone.

My eyes reluctantly open, and I realize I have stepped back into a nightmare. Except this now, is the reality. I am hesitant to leave the dream place where things are okay. I want to go back, and try to accept that I can't. The beeping and swooshing of machines are now undeniable. My heart sinks as it did the morning before.

Before being completely awake, I peek outside. I can see the sun trying to escape the clouds, and I relate. I am in a fog, trying to see clearly what has happened and where we go from here.

From a few feet away, Gavin quietly talks to the nurse "Can you wake up my mommy?" The nurse replies, "Of course sweetie, I can do that." But I am already making my way to him. It must be time for the new list of medications. I get up quickly, ignoring my wrinkled clothes and need for a shower.

Nothing matters in the same way that it has before. The past few days are a blur of tests, pokes, and medications. A constant stream of doctors continuously fills the room. As I walk over to Gavin he smiles and says, "Good morning Mommy. I hope you had a good rest!" His blue eyes shine with sincerity and he is expecting a smile.

He is the one who just had brain surgery, yet is making sure I had a good rest. Tears threaten to fall as I look at a new version of my son. Wires tangle around him and a constant drip of fluids hang by his bed.

I realize that although my heart physically hurts, Gavin needs me to be strong. I mirror his resilience and reply as if I have just had the most peaceful night of my life. "I did buddy. Are you being a brave boy taking your meds?"

I focus on Gavin's cheeks, a part of him that does not remind me of how things have changed so quickly. They are soft, innocent, and they remind me of when he was a baby, born so perfectly almost six years ago. I try to ignore the bandage that wraps around his head and the tube coming out of it draining cerebrospinal fluid. As much as I want to, I avoid staring into his big, blue eyes because they show the symptoms that brought us here.

There's an IV in Gavin's thin, fragile arm that drapes alongside of him and connects to the machines with their constant beeping. They are stealing the dreams I have for my child.

How did we get here?

I push this thought away just as quickly as it comes. Over time, it will be a necessary coping mechanism to pretend that my heart is not breaking. I cannot help but smile thinking of Gavin just a few days ago, at Grace's birthday party, doing headstands and flips. It gives me hope that maybe someday he will do it again.

Gavin smiles at me and asks for some root beer. He has always been good at tugging at my heartstrings when he wants something. I love that about him. I normally wouldn't let him have soda at 8 a.m., but things have changed. It was the easiest way for him to swallow the nine medications he had to take. I don't even quite understand what they are for, as I watch him ingest one after another.

The nurse, a cheerful young woman with long brown hair and a caring smile, cheers Gavin on until the medication tray is full of empty syringes. As she cleans up she says, "Gavin, you are such a trooper!" He shrugs his shoulders with a smirk. When she leaves he asks me "Mom why do people keep saying I'm a trooper? I don't even know what that is!" He is so funny and sarcastic, and makes me laugh when I want to cry.

I tell him that a trooper is like an army soldier who has to fight hard to reach a goal—to win a fight. He nods his head slowly, brows scrunched, considering whether he fits the criteria. "All right." he says.

Gavin's life has been turned upside down. He is now hooked up to IVs and recovering from brain surgery, but chooses to go with the flow.

Thank God he was a trooper from the beginning, as his battle had just begun.

Nicole Pierson

Chapter One

IT WAS APRIL in Minnesota. Every year at this time, we contemplate whether or not we should trust the spring weather and plan an outside party for Grace or if we should play it safe. Mother Nature hasn't decided if winter is over, or if spring has begun. Sometimes spring has been skipped altogether and we go straight into the hot, humid days of summer. This particular April happened to be very warm, thus our decision was easy. In the garage, Steve and I discuss where we should hang a piñata. "Can't you just tie it there?" I point up as Steve walks over with a small ladder.

"No, I will just put a rope around the rafter. That way, I can leave it up high until we are ready for it and then pull this side down," he explains. A soft breeze blows into the garage, carrying the wonderful aroma of the newly blossomed lilac tree from across the street. Spring has always been my favorite time of year. I know summer is around the corner and am so excited to spend time with the kids before they grow up. It seems their growing up is happening entirely too fast.

Gavin plays with cars in the driveway as Grace and Gage run around with Karma, our almost two-year-old yellow Lab. They keep running to the playhouse, which is atop a shed. As they run up to the top, Karma wags her tail in excitement, waiting at first and then following along. The kids scream with joy as she runs quickly to catch up with them.

Steve recently finished the playhouse, complete with stairs and a front porch. It is the best playhouse I have ever seen. It has electricity for the front porch light and there is talk of making a zip line from the deck of the house to the playhouse in order to send snacks. We have big plans. For the playhouse, for the weekend, and for our future.

Steve does the practical planning for events like these. He decides where the tables and chairs should go, and other logistics that I don't always consider. I orchestrate the details about decorations, invitations, the theme of the day, and ordering the cake. Having three children four years apart has taught us to be a team. I tend to remember when the field trip slips are due, or when the cell phone needs to be paid. Steve does yard work and keeps the house up and running. He always opens biscuit containers for me because the anticipation of when they will pop open drives me crazy. I hate not knowing when they will pop.

Gavin does not have a care in the world as he plays. He is just a normal kid—a funny, active, sweet and sarcastic, normal kid. He loves kindergarten and learns something new each day. Other than strep a few times, Gavin has never been sick. He has never had any concerning symptoms until now.

As I sweep the garage floor, Steve asks, "Have you noticed Gavin has been opening his eyes really wide lately?" I pause to consider if I have. "Maybe he has allergies," I suggest.

I really hadn't noticed anything and was now curious. My mom has always had horrible allergies so it's possible.

"Hey buddy can you come over here for a minute?" I ask calmly as not to worry him or jump to conclusions. He drives his toy cars over to me, still kneeling on the garage floor. When I call his name again, he moves his head up and opens his eyes widely. He has a huge grin on his face, as he normally does. His eyes seem to be bothering him a little, but he didn't complain about anything. He just rubbed one and squinted the other as he continued to look up at us.

Knowing his silly and entertaining spirit, we simply noted it and went on with preparing for the big party. If it continues, I will bring him in next week. Surely, it didn't require additional worry at this time. I would watch it, I thought to myself. He continued on with playing, rubbing his eyes periodically. Within a couple of minutes, he was running outside with Grace, Gage and Karma.

Life continued.

AT 4:30 P.M. we had to get to Gavin's bi-weekly gymnastics class which is about a fifteen-minute drive. It was my turn to bring him so after I helped him get ready, he ran ahead of me to the car. "I'll be back around seven, please make sure the kids do not destroy the house while I'm gone," I say to Steve as I am backing out of the driveway. I had been cleaning the house for two days, and a two-year-old could easily undo that in an hour. "Decorating to be continued," I think to myself. As I drive away, I am making a mental to-do list. Finish decorations, cut fruit, tell Steve about the cake—wait did I order the cake? I remind myself that everything will work out as it has before.

Car rides with Gavin are never dull. He uses this time to school me on dinosaur facts or pose questions that are well beyond his years. Today was no different. "Mom, do you know what the largest dinosaur was?" I reply expectantly, "A T.rex?" Through the rear-view mirror, the look on his face tells me I am wrong.

"Mom, the biggest dinosaur is Argentinosaurus, but many people believe T.rex is one of the largest dinosaurs. Actually, a T.rex was only about thirteen feet tall." He speaks with such clarity and intelligence. I am about to change the conversation, but he is not finished. "T.rex isn't even the largest carnivore. Spinosaurus and Giganotosaurus are the largest carnivores." I smile at him as I often do and I tell him "Gavin you are so smart!"

Gavin did not waste time and always learned quickly. At eight and a half months, he started walking. Crawling was simply not allowing him to keep up with his big sister. He was early for nearly every milestone. He talked early, had amazing balance and hand-eye coordination, allowing him to ride a two-wheel bike at age four. He had an amazing memory and was a sponge, especially if it piqued his interest. As a teacher, I knew the importance of this natural curiosity. I had never worried for his future. His vocabulary was extensive. If he didn't know a word, he would keep that word in his memory until he could ask me what it meant. When I would ask him where he heard the word, he remembered exactly where and when. Besides being ahead developmentally and cognitively, he was very agile and strong which is why he loved gymnastics.

I sat with the other moms, watching our boys hang, climb and flip. Rose, another mom, comments on how funny Gavin is. I tell her "Yeah, you should have seen him last week, he was dancing for all of the team girls in the middle of a circle." I never knew what Gavin was planning, but he always was around to make an impression. If there wasn't entertainment, he was it.

I hear his coach say, "Nice job Spider Man," which has been his nickname since he started gymnastics at three. Slowly and reluctantly, I start to notice that he seems a little off. I try to ignore it but it persists. Normally, Gavin would run constantly without tiring, whether he was flipping, jumping or climbing the thirty-foot rope. This evening however, his eyes kept watering and he kept coming over to me saying he was tired. I encouraged him to keep going, thinking he just needed a nap or had a long day. With kindergarten and gymnastics twice a week, he was tired—I convinced myself. If I only knew, I would have been on my way to a hospital.

I hugged him and said, "It's okay Gav, practice is done in just ten minutes, and, if you can finish, I will buy you a gumball on our way out." He wipes his tears and says "Okay mom, I will try." I worry that he is getting a cold and hope he doesn't miss out on his sister's seventh birthday party or Easter this weekend. Even though he wasn't feeling well, he found strength somewhere deep down to keep going. I was trying to be the supportive mom, pushing him a little to not give up. I did not know how much his perseverance and attitude to keep going that night would be exactly what he needed in the coming days, and years, to follow.

As we drive home, the sun shines on my face and I can see Gavin's blonde hair and blue eyes in the rear-view mirror. His hair is so bright that it is almost white. Many times strangers have commented on his "towhead." Gavin cheerfully smiles at me and says, "Mom, thank you for the gumball!" He was so proud of himself for earning that gumball, and he thoroughly enjoyed it as children often do with the small things in life.

WHEN I OPEN the door, I see Grace trying to decorate the wall with crepe paper. It is all twisted and falling. She looks at me and says "Mom, I was going to surprise you!" I walk over while simultaneously assessing her progress, knowing she has the best of intentions but needs help. Together, we unravel the crepe paper and start over. Gavin is gone, and I hear the boys, Steve included, wrestling around. Gage is yelling, "No, not the claw!" and Gavin is coming to his rescue.

I peek my head around the corner to where they wrestle relentlessly, laughing and squealing about. I smile. Steve knows when some fun is in order and he helps me see the power of laughter and playing. I love that about him. The kids beg him to tickle them, throw them in the air or wrestle around. He can't say no.

Gavin must be feeling better. He is showing Steve what he learned at gymnastics and jumping from couch to couch. After about twenty minutes, they all call a fair truce. Steve walks by Grace and me, and glances at our under-the-sea efforts with the crepe paper. We have alternated light and dark blue twirls from top to bottom on the wall. Behind the crepe paper are various sea creatures. "Nice job, ladies," he says as he puts his shoes on to mow the lawn before it is dark.

It has been a long day. After decorating and much needed baths, I read to Grace while Steve puts the boys to bed in their bunk bed. I look at my sweet little girl. "You are such an amazing girl Gracie, you know that right?" She smiles. I cannot believe she is seven. Where has the time gone, I wonder to myself while I stroke her beautiful blonde hair behind her ear.

"Get some sleep sweet girl, I love you," I whisper as I kiss her forehead. As I make my way to bed, I stop by the boys' room to say good night. They are already sleeping and look exhausted. I close their door carefully and head upstairs.

As I finally place my head on my pillow I do another mental checklist. I go through every detail. I lean over to Steve and ask, "What time are you going to pick up the cake tomorrow?"

"I'll get it when I run to get ice, around noon babe, don't worry," he replied while kissing me on the cheek.

He knows I need to have a plan. He often tells me not to worry, knowing it's innately something I have always done. It's a mom thing. Or maybe just my personality. As I close my eyes and envision our weekend of celebration, I feel like I have planned for everything.

My world is still and calm. I begin to drift to sleep unknowing of what tomorrow will bring, planning for events I think will happen and not for what is soon to transpire. For the last night in my life, I have peace that my children are safe and I can keep them that way.

Abruptly, everything I thought I knew, was going to change.

Chapter Two

Be on your guard; stand firm in the faith;
be courageous; be strong.

1 Corinthians 16:13

BIRDS ARE CHIRPING and the bright sun is pushing through my bedroom window. I lay there a minute, knowing that once I rise, I will be going all day long. I can hear little feet across the kitchen floor and living room downstairs. As I walk down, Grace jumps up and down "Mom I can't wait for my parties today!" Gavin comes up to my leg, wrapping one arm around it, "I love you, Mommy." As I begin pouring cereal for the kids, I watch Gavin carefully. I see that he is rubbing his eyes more than yesterday.

In light of his behavior at gymnastics last night I am beginning to grow concerned about his eyes. Nothing else seems to be bothering him but I am on high alert. I will watch him—I think to myself as I take out food to prepare for the party. I lure the kids downstairs, "Dad set up a tent in the playroom! You should go play so Mommy can get everything ready."

Before I could finish my sentence, they all simultaneously bolt towards the basement door. "I'll beat you there!" Gavin challenges. Grace is right with him and Gage trails behind. I wince and inhale as I hear them march down the stairs, hoping they don't miss a step or end up trampled on top of each other. A few seconds later, I exhale, hearing they made it down safely. ER trip avoided. Steve comes in from the garage and sees me busy in the kitchen. "I'll play with them to keep them out of your hair," he says, knowing how helpful this will be. I move about the kitchen without missing a beat. I have two hours until Grace's friends arrive. "Thanks, hon," I reply gratefully.

"IT'S TIME MOM!" Grace declares. She is excited to have girls from her class over before having family come celebrate later. I do one more walk through of the house, making sure one of the boys has not left a dirty sock, or something worse, on display. The boys are playing Mario™ on the Wii™ downstairs and everything looks and smells inviting. Mission accomplished. The front living room looks like the ocean. The doorbell rings and Grace's friends come in one after another. While Grace and her friends giggle and play, Gavin entertains them, jumping around and being his normal sarcastic, hilarious self. He is showing off his newest skill, a head stand, and he does it well. As I take a picture of Grace and her friends, Gavin photobombs the picture and hops in at the last second. He was acting completely normal. He always loved being around the girls and they always loved him too.

After two hours of seven-year-old girls, I was ready for some adults to arrive. I have three sisters and two brothers, as well as many close aunts, cousins, and friends, so we always have more than a full house. As a child, my parents always held big celebrations for our birthdays, so I have continued the tradition.

In attendance at the family party was Lisa, my aunt who is a pediatrician and who previously worked at the National Institute of Health (NIH). She is always our go-to person when we have medical concerns—usually on stuff like ear infections or if she's lucky, the occasional TMI conversation with Grandpa. Bless her soul. Little ones are constantly sick, so I was always asking. She has been an invaluable resource and I have always trusted her opinion. I planned on asking her about Gavin's eyes and allergies when an opportunity presented.

I notice Steve casually asking her to take a look at Gavin, and explaining his behavior over the past couple of days. I was busy making sure everyone had enough to eat, and also visiting with other family and friends. Controlled chaos ensues. The adults are chatting while the children are running from outside to downstairs to the playhouse and yard, constantly asking for cake and ice cream.

I make my way over to Steve as Lisa is doing some kind of exam, having Gavin follow her finger with his eyes. Gavin stands there impatiently, wanting to run away and get to the important playing stuff. As I watch, the look on Lisa's face was concerned, yet calm. It appeared that Gavin could not look up, and that his left eye was not tracking with his right eye. As she showed me what she meant, I could see that his eyes were worse than the day before, and that the left eye was not moving as fast or as far as the right.

She explains to me that there are nerves behind the eyes which could cause these symptoms with increased pressure. She was careful about what she said but recommended we leave the birthday party and head straight to Children's Hospital in St. Paul. She delicately answered my questions as to what would cause these symptoms—I believe to spare me from unnecessary worry. We decided to quickly sing Happy Birthday, eat cake, and prepare a bag just in case we were admitted to the hospital. I casually started to clean up the cake mess, knowing I had to go. Maybe if I prolong it, I would somehow change what I was about to hear.

While I serve the cake, my mom says, "I will stay to clean up, everyone understands if you have to go." I agree with her that we should probably get going. The remaining family stayed and finished the party. Steve, Gavin, and I got into the minivan and were on our way to St. Paul, about a forty-five-minute drive.

As we drive on interstate 94, I stare out the window, my mind racing through different scenarios. I turn to Steve, who is driving and ask "What do you think is wrong with his eyes?" "I don't know," he replies. We agree how devastating it would be if Gavin needed some kind of eye surgery, and also the worst case scenario we could imagine at that time, if Gavin were to go blind.

Gavin loved nature and science. He has always had an interest in all animals, dinosaurs and especially sea creatures. From the time he could talk, he was learning facts about the world around him. Since Gavin was three, he has wanted to be a marine biologist when he grows up. The thought that he may need a surgery and that his eyes could be damaged was a difficult picture for us. I shake my head slowly imagining this and whisper, "If Gavin couldn't see the world, his dreams and joy would be gone." Steve agrees. I was heartsick by this thought and had the sudden urge to fast forward to a diagnosis.

Thoughts of what could be wrong flood my mind as we continue towards St. Paul. I continue to worry about blindness. I think about how many times Gavin has noted a beautiful sunset and how he carefully watches the animals at the zoo. He soaks up everything around him, through his eyes. I silently pray that his eyes will be okay.

I look back at Gavin and he smiles, a carefree smile that every child deserves to have. As we neared Children's Hospital, we were concerned, but had confidence the doctors would figure it out and fix it. I calm my fears by recalling the time Grace couldn't breathe from croup and they gave her a steroid injection. She went home and recovered. I recall Gage's traumatic birth and short stay in the NICU, and all of the times I brought the kids in for ear infections, strep, or the flu. They all ended well, and this will too, I thought.

As we exit to downtown St. Paul, I think about the times I had been there before. It is such a beautiful city. Many times I've been here for events at the Xcel Energy Center, the Science Museum, the Children's Museum, and fun outings with friends. Good memories, I think to myself.

The hospital is connected to many other clinics, surgery centers, medical buildings and United Hospital. "I had no idea such a large complex was right here next to the Xcel," I say to Steve.

We follow the signs for the emergency department and pull into the red parking ramp at 5:00 p.m. We proceed to registration. Gavin stops before getting onto the elevator, "Why are we here? Will it take a long time?" I hug him and say, "We want to figure out why your eyes are bothering you. Hopefully, it will be quick."

"Can we go back to the party after?" he asks with hope in his voice.

"We'll see bud. We just have to make sure everything is okay with your eyes," Steve tells him.

Gavin wanted to get this sorted out so that he could get back to being a five-year-old. We promised him that the Easter Bunny would come tonight and that once we figured out what was going on, we would go home and get ready for our Easter festivities. I learned that night, I no longer had the ability to promise anything to Gavin.

As I walk up to the registration window, a woman greets us and asks if we need to be seen. Steve and Gavin head to the waiting area as I begin to explain why we are here. I explain Gavin's watery eyes and how they recently seemed to be having trouble with movement and control.

I follow that quickly with saying, "If it wasn't Saturday, I would have made an appointment with his pediatrician," as if it was not really an emergency. Likely because that is what I desperately wanted to believe.

"Here is some paperwork we need you to fill out, and while you are doing so I will make a copy of his insurance card," she tells me. I leave Gavin's card and take the clipboard, heading over to Steve and Gavin who are staring into the fish tank. Gavin looks up at me excitedly and says, "I see Dori from Finding Nemo!" I look with interest, as if he had just made the most amazing discovery. I love his excitement for nature and animals and can easily picture him growing up and being a marine biologist, just as he has planned.

The waiting area is spacious, and we are only in it with one other child and his father. The walls are brightly painted with stars, calming pictures hung neatly. Gavin walks by the other child and says hello but it does not appear he speaks English. Realizing this, he walks past him to grab a book from the shelf, and returns to my lap.

Gavin always attempts to make friends. He sees good in every person. He is gentle, loving and loyal. As he sits on my left knee reading, I continue with the paperwork on the right:

"Is your child on any medications?" No.
"Does your child have asthma?" No.
"Was your child born full term?" Yes.
"List any hospitalizations your child has had." None.
"Does your child have any medical conditions?" No.
"Comments/Concerns?" Gavin is a healthy child, who recently began experiencing watery eyes and tracking problems. Slight fatigue.

I finish fairly quickly and bring the paperwork back to the nurse. I hope we can see the doctor soon, who I figure will refer us to some type of eye specialist whom we can see next week. My mind never stops planning and preparing. I wonder if my house is still as messy as it was when I left so abruptly, and think about the Easter baskets I still need to assemble.

Nicole Pierson

About ten minutes pass and we are called to the nurse check-in area, a small office behind the registration window. Gavin sits down as she checks his heart rate, blood pressure and temperature. I explain to the nurse that this just started within the past few days. I also tell her, other than the eye symptoms, he seemed to be tired and emotional last night at gymnastics.

She leads us to a room and within about twenty minutes a doctor knocks on the door. "Come in!" we both say invitingly. I think to myself, that was fast for an ER, hopefully that means we won't be here all night. The young looking doctor is calm and approachable. He sits down at the end of the bed and Gavin moves his head to the right so he can see the cartoons. "So what brings you here tonight?" he asks. I repeat what we told the nurse. "Has he had any headaches, nausea or dizziness?" The answer is no. I assume those symptoms exist when there is a problem with eyes. Why else would he be asking?

He asks Gavin to follow his finger and tells us there is something going on. He makes a few notes, and tells us he will return shortly to have another doctor take a look. We look at each other slightly concerned. Gavin is looking at us, trying to figure out why our faces have changed and what it means. Steve assures him "They just need another doctor to see what your eyes are doing so they can fix it." Without taking his eyes off the TV, he shrugs his shoulders and says, "Okay."

The room was small, but kid friendly, with bright blue and green walls and a nice flat screen TV. There is a gentle but urgent knock on the door. We again invite them to come in, slightly more hesitant this time around. "Hello, I am the lead doctor tonight and I am just going to take a look at Gavin's eyes." He has a calm demeanor and walks over to Gavin with concern.

Gavin doesn't say much, wanting to get it over with. As he examines Gavin's eyes, he explains they are not moving properly. "You see, he is unable to look up which is called Parinaud's Syndrome, and this is usually caused by pressure of some sort." He goes on to tell us he would like to do a CT scan to see what may be causing that pressure. Although we were worried, we tried to stay calm. I did not understand what could cause pressure or this new symptom. An infection or eye disease was my best guess.

A mass in the center of my child's brain never entered my mind.

We tell Gavin the doctors need to take a picture of his head, and it will only take a few minutes. His biggest worry is if he could come back to the toys in the room and we assured him he could. A few minutes pass and the radiology nurse comes in to get Gavin. He hops off the bed and cheerfully walks to the radiology unit. Without fear, he lays down very still while they take a couple of pictures. Steve and I are next to Gavin telling him he's doing a great job. The techs who are viewing the pictures from behind the glass have a concerned look on their face that I try not to notice.

I consider that I'm probably reading their nonverbal language wrong, maybe they are just trying to get a better picture. After all, many times before, I had brought my little ones to urgent care, sure it was some life-threatening situation, and it turned out to be a cold or a virus. Steve and I are quiet as the radiology tech tells us he is done and can go back to his room.

Nicole Pierson

"Good job Gavin, you sat so nice and still," I say as we walk back. "There's our room!" Gavin excitedly says as we round the corner. The radiology nurse tells us the doctor will review the scan and be in with results soon, and leaves us to wonder what's next.

A FEW MINUTES later, a nurse comes in with some pajamas for Gavin to put on. She explains to us that they are more comfortable and it's getting late, about 8:00 p.m. now. They were adorable light blue cotton pajamas that look fairly comfortable. I feel like all signs are pointing to something bad about to happen, yet I keep pushing these thoughts away. We sit in silence, waiting for the doctors to give us the results. I feel like I have signed up for sky-diving and just before I am ready to jump, I change my mind. Can't I just go home, back to safety? Hello, can anyone hear me? I don't want to jump!

But it was too late.

We have been waiting expectantly for that knock. With every passing minute, I feel like it is more serious than we anticipated.

Gavin looks innocent and vulnerable in his new attire. A child life specialist, named Dagny—lets him choose a stuffed animal while he waits so patiently. He chooses a blue bunny and quickly names him Hoppy. Surely Hoppy would keep him safe, he tells us. Gavin hugs his new companion, as Steve and I sit in silent apprehension. Dagny is upbeat and all smiles, helping this time of uncertainty pass by. She asks Gavin what he likes and says she will be back with some activities for him. The minutes following seem to play in slow motion.

The door handle turns firmly but cautiously as the two doctors open the door and walk in. I am no longer feeling so inviting. I'm actually feeling quite sick. I carefully watch their expressions and movements. They both sit down and explain that they have the results of the CT.

I inhale as I listen closely.

The lead doctor looks at us and quietly says, *"There is a mass in Gavin's brain."*

For what seemed to be forever I replay that sentence trying to understand that he was talking about my child. This feeling is strangely familiar. Like when I was in a car accident and one second I was driving and the next I wasn't. My brain could not gather all of the information to know what to do next.

I am suddenly lost somewhere in between knowing where I was going and being halted to a stop. After a few seconds, I begin to understand the world that has shifted around me.

I cannot breathe. There must be a mistake.

This five-year-old sitting on the bed next to us, playing with his new bunny? The strong little gymnast who flips, runs, jumps, climbs? Gavin, *my son*, has a brain tumor? I cannot accept those words. Maybe the scans are wrong. Yet, the doctor continues to move his mouth and from what I gather he is giving me more information. This is real. Gavin has a brain tumor.

It is incomprehensible. I hold back tears, while a lump in my throat threatens to strangle me. It just keeps playing *"There is a mass in Gavin's brain."* I cannot exhale this time. Things are not okay. I feel as if I am going to be sick. I somehow manage to form words but am not sure if what is coming out is comprehensible. "Where is the tumor located? How large is it? What kind of tumor is it? Is it treatable?" The questions all seem to come out at once, and I can't process the answers.

I somehow gather it is in the pineal region (where is that?), that it appears solid and cystic (what does that mean?), and they will not know more until an MRI is done. I gather we are not leaving anytime soon.

I turn to Gavin and just cannot say the words to him. Thus far, he has been ignoring our quiet conversation. Steve manages to say, "Buddy, there is something in your brain— some extra stuff that doesn't need to be there." His innocent reaction puts me over the edge.

Gavin looks at all of us and cheerfully says, "Mom and Dad, I knew I had a big brain!" He goes on, "I am getting so smart in kindergarten and I could feel my brain growing all year." Thank God he doesn't understand what this means. I don't even know what it means. His interpretation brings about new emotions and I can no longer hold the tears. I can't do this in front of Gavin, and Steve knows it. He offers to stay while I leave the room.

As I OPEN the door, I already have blurry vision from the stream of tears. I don't know where I am going, and all I can see is bright lights and empty hallways. I am searching for something but can't think about what that is. My phone perhaps? A tissue? God?

This cannot be happening. Oh my God, this is happening. All I can manage to do is continually fight with what I know and what I want to believe. I slowly sit against a wall while my body shakes from the intense emotion and fear. "God, help me, help Gavin," I plead.

A comforting hand finds my shoulder and calms the uncontrollable movements. "You are in the best place, and we will take care of Gavin," the nurse says to me calmly. I cannot talk, only cry. A few minutes pass and I see Dagny enter Gavin's room. Steve greets me in the hallway with open arms and we cry together. We can barely speak other than repeating, "Oh my God...Why Gavin... No!"

The nurse takes us to a room where we can be together and comprehend what to do next. Our grief is too much. We sob, we hug, and we fall to our knees and pray. I have never felt such despair in my life. Our sweet, innocent boy has a brain tumor and we do not know anything about it yet—if it can be cured, or what this means for him and his future. We have so many unanswered questions.

I manage to find my cell phone in my purse and dial my mom, who has been waiting to hear an update since we left the party. The phone rings differently as I wait for her to answer. It echoes more loudly and each ring lasts longer. I don't want to have to say it again. I hear her pick up and all that I can say is, "Mom." I stop and cannot get the words to come out of my mouth. She replies, "What Nikki? What is it?" with worry in her tone.

After a pause and deep breath, I manage, "Gavin has a brain tumor." I cannot hear what she says, she is hysterical and crying. I hear her tell us she will be there as soon as possible. She has to tell Grace and Gage their brother won't be home for Easter, and even worse, he is very sick.

Did the room get smaller? It feels like the walls are closing in, suffocating us. Steve and I hug once more and agree that Gavin needs us, and that there will be plenty of time for crying. Right now, we need to get back to Gavin. It dawned on us that we don't know exactly what happens now, tonight. There is pressure, and fluid, and Gavin needs emergency surgery. We wipe our tears and breathe deep, yearning for strength as we re-enter Gavin's room.

They are prepping him for an IV as they need to draw labs. He will be sedated for an MRI and surgery to relieve pressure in his brain. The CT had not only revealed the tumor, but also increased ventricles, which meant the tumor was blocking cerebrospinal fluid from traveling to the spine. This is very dangerous and could cause brain damage, coma or death if untreated.

When we walk into his room, Gavin is laughing with Dagny and she is showing him some games as a distraction. Steve goes around the bed to be on the side closest to Gavin. I am on the other as they prepare to place the IV. Thanks to lidocaine cream, the poke is quick and painless. He is barely forty-five pounds and his veins were easy to find. I push my worries away because I am with Gavin. I tell him the doctors are going to fix him and everything will be all right. I desperately hope my words are true.

"God, please be with Gavin and give us strength," I pray as Gavin is wheeled away from us into an operating room for the first time in his life. As the doors close, I am left feeling as if I'm in the middle of a tornado. Everything is shifting so rapidly and I can't stop it. My sweet boy, I am so sorry. I can't stop it.

Nothing pointed to a brain tumor. I told the surgeon that Gavin was doing head stands today. He couldn't believe it. The last thing he said to me was, "I will take good care of him and you should expect this to take a couple hours." I keep focusing on his calmness and know Gavin is in good hands.

As we walk to the waiting room, Steve and I go through the questions the neurosurgeon asked us. The tumor being the size of a golf ball, it should have caused headaches, balance issues, dizziness. Steve and I agree that Gavin had none of this. How can he have such perfect balance and have a mass in the center of his brain?

The waiting room is dark and quiet. It is now after 10:00 p.m. My parents, Theresa, and Jen meet us to offer support. Theresa is my aunt and Jen is her daughter, my cousin. I didn't talk. I just paced back and forth until I felt weak and had to sit for a minute. I sat until I felt sick again and had to pace.

My mind continues to wonder when did this happen, despite knowing there were no signs. Not that it will change anything, but how could I have missed a brain tumor? I recall two occasions when I brought him to the clinic because he seemed to tire more easily than his sister did, his lymph nodes were always swollen, he was paler than my other children, and he had a small appetite. Both times, he was checked out, blood work was done and I was told he was a growing, perfect, and healthy boy. I just trusted if there was something wrong, it would have been discovered.

I cannot do this. How can I do this? This morning I had three healthy children and now one is in brain surgery. God, help me—this hurts too much.

After many hours, around 1:30 a.m., a nurse escorts us up to the Pediatric Intensive Care Unit (PICU), where Gavin will be cared for. We have to wait to see him until they

Nicole Pierson

have him situated. I yearn to hold his hand, sing to him and kiss his sweet cheeks.

The neurosurgeon briefly updates us. He was able to successfully get the drain placed in Gavin's ventricles. He explains this will need to remain in Gavin's brain until his ventricles are normal size. Gavin will need to be very still and careful over the next few days.

He tells me they completed a full brain and spine MRI and we will get results tomorrow.

"Thank you so much," I say as I shake his hand.

"You're welcome," he says before turning away.

Finally, a little after 2:00 a.m., we are escorted into Gavin's room. All eyes are on us, and I suddenly feel panicked again. As we move the curtain, I can see he is sleeping peacefully. I take deep breaths as I wash my hands with the foam at the door. There is a white bandage wrapped around his head, tubes everywhere and machines beeping. It's hard to take in.

I walk over slowly as the nurses tend to him. I glance at the bag at the end of the drain coming from Gavin's head. I realize the clear fluid is my child's brain fluid, and feel queasy.

I sit next to him and hold his hand. It is soft and warm. I whisper in his ear as I had countless times before:

You are my sunshine, my only sunshine.
You make me happy, when skies are gray.
You'll never know dear, how much I love you
Please don't take my sunshine away.

Grace and Gavin January 2012. Best friends,
singing and dancing on the stairs.

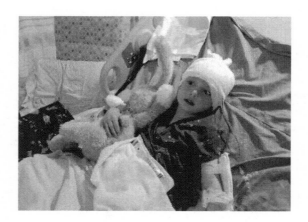

Gavin Easter 2012

Nicole Pierson

Chapter Three

All you need is the plan, the roadmap,
and the courage to press on to your destination.

Earl Nightingale

GAVIN'S JOURNEY BEGINS.

I manage to hold Gavin in my arms, avoiding the IVs and tubes. He sleeps like an angel on my lap, and after staring at him awhile, my eyes finally start to close. Steve helps me get him comfortable in his bed and I make my way to the couch bed. "Mommy will be right here Gav, I will never leave you," I whisper as I kiss him goodnight.

I couldn't mentally check a to-do list and fall asleep. Nothing was in order. My kids were not safe from pain. I am vulnerable and weak. Foolish for thinking something like this wouldn't happen to my child. Viewing the world now from a different lens, I had succumbed to the realization that I was not in control anymore. I never was.

Voices fill the room and I realize it's somehow morning already. There are people, I presume doctors, checking on Gavin. I nudge Steve to wake up and wipe the drool from the corner of my mouth. What a great first impression. As I stand up to introduce myself, I massage the kink in my neck and try to look alert. I sense the doctor doesn't care about how we look anyways. Her concern, thankfully, was for my child fighting a brain tumor.

"Hello, I am Gavin's mom, Nicole. Nice to meet you," I say as my brain comes into full focus. Steve follows suit as we all find a chair near Gavin's bedside.

"My name is Dr. Kris Ann Schultz and I am a pediatric oncologist," the doctor explains. The word oncologist does not sit well with me. I know the translation. Cancer doctor. As scary as this is, Dr. Schultz is calm, and listens to my every concern and question.

I explain what I thought I knew about the tumor and ask her to explain what it is, how it grew, and what we will do to treat it.

She thoughtfully explains that it's likely a germ cell tumor which means that Gavin was born with it. Germ cell tumors contain cells that should have gone to the reproductive organs during development, but some traveled midline up to the pineal region. This, I learned, is an area deep in the brain, under fluid-filled ventricles. The tumor grew slowly over the past almost six years, until it got so large it blocked fluid, causing the recent issues.

I ask what treatment will be given, and she explains once the biopsy and tumor markers are completed, a diagnosis will be more complete. Treatment could include chemotherapy, surgery, and radiation. It is a lot to take in, but she assures me we will have a plan soon.

Gavin mostly ignores us as he watches a movie. Dr. Schultz stands next to him and he shows her the dinosaur he is holding. Her dinosaur knowledge is extensive, apparent by her facts about Giganotosaurus. Gavin is thoroughly impressed and they have an instant connection. She shares that her son also loves dinosaurs. She is patient, nurturing, and kind.

The day is busy with so many doctors to meet and talk to. I am impressed so many are here on Easter. Gavin is cuddled with Hoppy, napping on and off.

He admires how the Easter bunny found him here at the hospital. "Wow, three Easter baskets!" he exclaims as he looks around his room. Child life specialists are health professionals that help children get through medical procedures, appointments, and hospital stays. Last night, a specialist brought baskets in for him while he slept. He thought he was the luckiest boy in the world—in the hospital, on Easter, with a brain tumor and recovering from brain surgery. Life is all about perspective.

His life has changed overnight, yet he is thankful he has three Easter baskets. With a tube coming out of his brain, he remains still as he's been told, as to not change the flow of the fluid. No complaints. Just happy.

I realize he may not fully understand the scope of his diagnosis. He does understand he's stuck in a bed all day though, and chooses to be happy. He had to leave his sister's birthday party and miss Easter. He is hooked up to machines and has to sit still so brain fluid does not drain too fast causing severe headaches and vomiting.

The ophthalmologist comes in to evaluate Gavin's eye changes. He explains that the pressure on the optic nerves is causing many things I cannot pronounce. Gavin is to wear an eyepatch to help his eyes strengthen. A pirate is born, and Gavin begins thinking of pirate names. So far, nothing is set in stone.

Family and friends went into support mode quickly. By the end of the day Gavin had eight Easter baskets, five DVDs, candy galore and many cards and activities to keep him busy. Many visitors came to see him. We knew we would be there awhile, so family helped out by bringing clothes, food, and activities for us.

Slowly, I could breathe. I knew we were not in this alone. No matter what, we have to keep putting one foot in front of the other. By the end of the day, we had met the ophthalmologist, the intensivist, the neuro-nurse practitioner, hospitalist and oncologist assigned to Gavin's care. If family was not present, doctors or specialists were—and usually it was at the same time.

The intensivist is the doctor on the floor of the intensive care unit. He allowed me to view the MRI scans and I got my first glimpse of the tumor. I just stared at it as if I could somehow make it disappear but there it was, in the middle of Gavin's brain.

It was about the size of a golf ball and had a few cystic parts but mostly solid. The cystic parts are honeycomb shaped and spread evenly throughout the mass. I was told it was well encapsulated, meaning it had defined borders and did not infiltrate surrounding tissues. That ball of cells was threatening my son's life.

Nicole Pierson

EVENING BRINGS A few more visitors. My grandpa Kenny, a veteran, walks in to see Gavin in the late afternoon. I have never seen him cry. He looks at Gavin and loses it. "But he's just a boy," he tells my grandma, his eyes filled with tears. Adults get cancer. But a child, a young spirited boy, should not.

Gavin's cousins come in to see him and what they see is a version of Gavin they have not seen before. I could tell they were afraid of all of the lines, bandages, machines. He slept as they held his hand or gave him cards.

Finally, the room is still. Steve and I sit in silence as Gavin rests. Well, a new type of silence where machines beep in a rhythm, while IVs drip, and not a word is spoken. The phone rings and Steve answers, "Okay, we will come out," I hear before he hangs up. Gage is too young to come into the PICU, he tells me. We decide to take turns going to the waiting area so Gavin is never alone.

As the double door clicks and opens, their blonde hair comes into sight. "Mommy!" Grace and Gage run to me. I hug them simultaneously, so tightly. My heart breaks for them, knowing Steve and I will be away for a-while. Gage is too little to understand, but Grace asks me, "Mom, is Gavin going to be okay?" Gavin and Grace are only thirteen months apart, and are best friends. How do I tell her how serious this is?

Last week they were running and playing, and now Gavin lays still in the intensive care unit. I open my mouth to answer, not sure of what will come out.

"Sweetie, Gavin has a tumor in his head and he needs medicine to get rid of it."

"Like grape medicine?" she innocently asks.

"Yes, sweetie, like that."

I wish that's all it was. Fever reducer, antibiotic— heck I would take stitches like the time Grace split her chin wide open at the end of the driveway. I wished so badly this could be an easy fix. I knew it wasn't.

I cuddle Gage a few minutes before he decides he wants to run. Grandpa Dan follows and I ask Grace if she wants to see Gavin.

We pick up the phone at the doors of the PICU, and wait. The doors open and Grace skips as she holds my hand. To her, this is an exciting new place and in her mind, doctors fix everything. No fear, until she sees her brother—her best friend in the state that he is.

Slowly, her expression changes. As she approaches the bed, I see her look at the bandage on his head, the tubes, and the machines. I see her go from excitement, to fear, to love. She walks to the other side of the bed and gives Gavin a hug on the arm that is not full of IVs.

"Happy Easter," she says quietly as she curiously looks around the room at all of the baskets. Shoot, I realize, I never made it home to assemble hers. We tell her the Easter bunny came here and we pick out the most girly of the bunch as her own. She then picks out a basket for Gage, who is likely still doing circles around Grandpa.

Steve hugs her tight as she sits on his lap. "I love you baby girl," he says. For a moment, as I watch them, I find myself feeling something other than sadness.

Back in the waiting area, I kissed my babies' goodbye, not knowing when I would see them again. I know they are loved and will be cared for. I block the guilt, because my brain can only process so much emotion at one time.

Nicole Pierson

As the sun sets and the lights dim in the hallways of the PICU, the intensivist walks in giving us information for tomorrow's needle biopsy. It is scheduled along with a third ventriculostomy, which will help drain fluid from the ventricular system to the spine. This will eventually eliminate the drain coming out of his ventricles.

"We have to be awake by 6:00 a.m. for his biopsy," I say to Steve as he starts to make our bed. For the past two hours, we have each been reading or typing to friends and family. We occasionally interact but mostly cope by distraction. We attempt to fold the couch out to a full-size bed, and, thanks to a nurse, are successful. Slowly, we are learning to accommodate to hospital life.

Nighttime is tough. Sometimes my mind will just not shut off! With three kids, it is sometimes the only time I can hear myself think. Today was so busy and I was trying to process all of the medical jargon. I have so many unanswered questions and fears about Gavin's future and cannot stop my thoughts.

This is really happening, Gavin is having a second brain surgery and he may have cancer and there is nothing I can do to stop it. My thoughts continue until my body demands rest and somehow I fall asleep.

OUR FIRST ENCOUNTER with Dr. Petronio happens bedside, while Gavin sleeps. Dr. Petronio is the head of neurosurgery at both St. Paul and Minneapolis Children's Hospitals. Before meeting him, I was nervous. After all, he is a brain surgeon who will be opening my son's head. As he walks in, calmly and purposefully, I feel instantly less worried.

Dr. Petronio brings with him an aura of confidence. Talking brain surgery with him is easier than I anticipated. I am learning new vocabulary like shunt, ventriculostomy, cerebrospinal fluid. Brain surgery does not seem so scary. He explains that the needle biopsy is minimally invasive and the ventriculostomy is a small procedure to allow fluid to drain. He expects the surgery to last a couple of hours.

I feel at ease as Dr. Petronio leaves. There is something about his demeanor, his presence.

I am allowed to go into the operating room as Gavin is wheeled into surgery. I am wearing a gown, cap and mask, as I hold Gavin's hand. As they are injecting the medicine to sedate him, Dr. Petronio asks him what he plans on dreaming about during the surgery.

"I am going to dream about getting out of here," he says with a smirk.

Laughter fills the OR. The surgical team has experienced Gavin—the boy who makes everyone laugh before having brain surgery!

We are escorted to the same waiting room as we were two nights before—the night we were told our healthy child had a life-threatening disease. That moment changed the course we were on and continues to replay in my mind. Our sweet boy is now having his second surgery since this began less than forty-eight hours ago. Steve and I hold hands and sit quietly. I silently pray. Steve has not always believed or been certain in a God. He hopes there is, but has not been convinced, I guess. He went through the steps of confirmation and we married in a church, but he still questioned his faith.

So I prayed myself. And we waited.

Nicole Pierson

Our family is not with us today. My uncle Bob, who was sick for a couple of years, passed away last week and today is his funeral. I am missing his funeral because my five-year-old is having brain surgery.

We are on hold. Our life, our plans, our thoughts. We watch mindless TV, speak a few words here and there, but mostly we just sit and wait.

Inhale and wait.

The doors from the surgery center make a clicking sound when they are about to open. Every time I hear that sound, my heart skips a beat and my head turns to see if it is Dr. Petronio. Finally, a couple of hours later, it was.

He sat down next to us and told us that Gavin is doing well, and that he was able to get a couple of tissue samples. The samples were sent to pathology and we will hear in the next few days, what type of tumor this is.

"Were you able to get a good look at it?" Steve asks.

"Yeah, I did. It is very dense and the tissue is not soft," he explains.

He tells us that he would not feel comfortable doing surgery on it yet, because of the size, composition and location. He explains he hopes chemotherapy can shrink it some and then he would try to remove it. We thanked Dr. Petronio for everything and went back to the PICU where Gavin was recovering.

Exhale. Gavin had another brain surgery under his belt. We finally felt some relief that the biopsy results would give us some sort of plan. For the next few days, we read messages of hope from friends and family via text messages, emails, Facebook and Gavin's Caring Bridge journal. When I would feel anxious, writing was my lifeline. I could type out my worst fears, my unbelievable realities, and then take care of Gavin.

Gavin got used to taking many medications each day. He had swelling from the tumor, and needed steroids. I have never experienced the effects of steroids. The only thing I knew about them was that athletes get into trouble for using them to build muscle. I had no idea that they reduce inflammation and are often given to brain tumor patients. For the first time ever, our thin boy was hungry all the time. He thought he could order "room service," as he called it, all day long.

By the fourth day, Gavin was moved from PICU to the medical surgery floor. He took advantage of the continued "room service," massages, and nurses. He told them how nice they were, and how he liked their voices, and many more charming things. Travis, a nurse Gavin had in PICU, came to check on him on the floor often after his shift. Gavin and Travis were instant buddies. He knew what Gavin needed, distracted him from the pain and just connected in a special way while Gavin was in his care. I am touched he is taking time to check on him. The amount of compassion we have seen is amazing. Although we were in the hospital, in a situation we never imagined we would be in, Gavin was okay. He was making the best out of every experience. At five, he was handling this better than most adults.

He uses humor to make situations better. One night, the machine for his IV kept beeping and the nurse kept trying to fix it. After about the fifth time she came in, he looks at her and says, "It is just not your night." We both laughed so hard. Where does he come up with this stuff?

Nicole Pierson

IT'S DAY SEVEN. We learned today that the biopsy showed a germ cell tumor called a mature teratoma, a benign tumor. The treatment for this would be surgery alone. However, the bloodwork showed a slight increase in AFP (Alpha Fetoprotein) levels. This could mean it was partially cancerous. The final diagnosis is a "mixed pineal region nonseminomatous germ cell tumor," or for short "pineal NSGCT." The diagnosis meant we could go home soon and start fighting this thing. Our fear was temporarily distracted with a plan.

Dr. Schultz gave us the roadmap. It was a piece of paper that essentially laid out all scenarios and action steps based on how treatment went. The plan was to do six rounds of chemotherapy, surgery to remove residual tumor, and out-of-state proton beam radiation. I kept reminding myself to breathe as I looked at the piece of paper in my hand. This is different than the summer I had planned. It is overwhelming to look too far ahead, so I remind myself to focus on right now.

As we read through the list of side effects from chemo, we knew them all too well. Ten years ago, just weeks before our wedding, Steve went to the doctor after finding a lump. At twenty-three years of age, he was not overly concerned but was due for a physical anyways. This visit ended in a testicular cancer diagnosis. The doctors said it was very aggressive and did surgery to remove the mass days later. It had already spread to his lymph nodes in his abdomen. It would have gone to major organs next. It was considered Stage II.

Steve started chemo just four weeks before our wedding. A few days before we said our vows, his hair came out in clumps and he decided to shave it all off. He was not sad for himself, but for me—worried he would ruin our wedding pictures. He had hoped to keep his hair until after the wedding. I told him that day how much I loved him, not his hair—that in the place of hair in those pictures, would be love and hope. He found an awesome cowboy hat and wore it at the wedding. He showed me what courage was, and never felt sorry for himself.

Thankfully, we saw the good side of chemo, and after four months, Steve was cured. He was able to take time off from work as a carpenter, thanks to Aflac coverage he had. He slowly gained weight again, felt well and after a few months we finally went on our honeymoon. We thought that if we got through that, we could tackle anything life throws our way. Chemo, in our experience, was worth the side effects. It made him sick and lose his hair, but he is here because of it. So as we read through the list of side effects, we assured Dr. Schultz that we were well aware and wanted to proceed. Surely it would shrink this tumor, we thought, and Gavin will go back to his life. That was our experience before.

After eight long days, Gavin's nurse is helping us prepare to go home. For a couple of days, we will escape the hospital. The bandage from Gavin's head is now gone, and there are two scars reminding us of what has happened. But he is still my Gavin and he is coming home.

Temporary joy washed over me. We are going home and we have a plan. There some order restored in our universe.

When we step outside, the air was fresh and new. It was a little cool, but the sun warmed Gavin's face. He just closed his eyes and soaked it in. I felt like I was experiencing outside air for the first time. Just breathing it in and out of my lungs gave me a new perspective. This air, something that is needed to sustain my life, is right here, readily available. I could breathe again. Gavin is here, breathing it too. Right now, in this moment, he is okay.

Life can change in an instant, and standing here breathing is a gift, I realize.

We hadn't given Gavin too many details at this point as far as treatment goes. We told him that he would be going back a few times to get rid of this tumor. He just wanted to be home and move on with life, yet understood he would be back. He looked at Steve and me as we drove away and said, "I know you will keep me safe."

LIFE WAS NOW uncertain, but love was not. How amazing a child could understand that. Despite all that had happened, he continued to believe in us to fight for him and protect him.

The drive home was quiet and calm. Gavin peacefully stared out the window, one eye covered by an eye patch. He did finally agree on a pirate name. Captain No Beard was what Gavin came up with. However, Steve had a different one. Gavin wore a hospital gown throughout his stay, and Steve thought that Captain No Pants was more fitting. Two pirate names it is.

Steve and Gavin are so much alike. They lighten my life. The eye patch could have been a constant reminder of the power of the brain tumor that is pushing on his brain and causing issues. Instead, they used it as a reminder that life is what you make of it.

When we got home, our house was clean and stocked with meals and snacks from family and friends. I had my family together in the comforts of our home. There was no beeping. Gavin bravely told his siblings how tough he was in the hospital, and that he is a trooper. Naturally, he explained what that was and also informed them he was Captain No Beard, a.k.a Captain No Pants.

As I fell asleep that night, in my own bed, it felt different. I had lost and gained so much in just eight days. I lost blissful ignorance and gained the ability to view life as the precious gift it is.

For tonight, I had my family back together again, and that was all that mattered.

I am cuddling with my three children under one roof. Simple pleasures I took for granted. We would be soon bringing Gavin back in for another procedure that would prep him for chemo, but for now we were together.

Chapter Four

Be strong and courageous.
Do not fear or be in dread of them,
for it is the LORD your God who goes with you.
He will not leave you or forsake you.

Deuteronomy 31:6

GAVIN IS RESTING, something he does often these days. Soon I will have to wake him for 2:00 p.m. meds. Grace and Gage are playing outside so it's quiet. Occasionally I go outside and play kick ball with them, before coming back to in to check on Gavin. As I walk over to him, the scar is what I see first. I hyper focus on it, feeling my heart beat faster. I kiss his forehead and remind myself he is okay right now. He's not playing outside, but he's okay.

On the counter, next to his T-ball schedule was a purple shirt. On the back was "Gavin #1." I stared at it, frozen for a moment. He had played the two years before, and was supposed to begin last week. His coach had brought him his shirt last week while in the hospital. When I unpacked our hospital bags, I threw his shirt on the counter, without much thought. Now just looking at it, has me nearly in tears. At this point, Gavin has double vision and cannot move his eyes upward. After eight days in the hospital, he is a little weak. The new medicines have side effects. I doubt Gavin will make it to a game this year, unless he is on the sidelines. It crushes me. This is so unfair.

I've created a medicine schedule so that I won't forget anything. Yesterday, I talked with Gavin's school about homebound services, which he will start next week. His kindergarten teacher will come after school twice a week. Today I spent the morning on the phone with Medica and scheduled Gavin's next round of appointments. It is a full time job coordinating everything.

I applied for a leave of absence from teaching and Steve continued to work as a carpenter, while also finishing school to be a police officer, something he always wanted to do. Family and friends were planning benefits to help with medical costs. We adapted our lives around Gavin's treatment. We were ready to follow the map, and had an adorable pirate on board to lead us.

The procedure we need to soon bring Gavin in for is to add a port and G-tube. The port gives an easy access to a vein so IVs and labs could be done easily, and the G-tube was placed to give nutrition if Gavin did not eat during his treatment. He was very thin at diagnosis and we knew he couldn't afford to lose any weight.

Nicole Pierson

With every adjustment we make to accommodate this brain tumor, the life Gavin had slips away. He should be wearing his purple jersey, running bases. He should be playing outside and climbing trees. He is fighting to live. My emotions take over until slowly I am sobbing into the jersey he will never wear. I've learned to sob quietly when emotions wash over me unexpectedly. I refuse to give into fear in front of my children. I choose to fill them up with hope. I bring the baseball shirt to Gav's room, fold it up nicely and put it on his shelf. Just like the rest of his dreams, there it will stay for now.

AFTER A FEW days of normalcy, Gavin is scheduled to have his port and G-tube surgeries. I help him get his shoes on and tears begin to fall off his sweet face. His head is down and he is quiet.

"What's wrong, Gav?" I ask.

"Mom, I don't want to go back into the hospital," he says with compliance, knowing he doesn't have a choice. It took everything not to cry with him. Up to this point, he hasn't been sad about this new life. I want to tell him I will cancel it and we can cuddle on the couch. I want to tell him this was all a bad dream. But I can't. So I get on my knees and wipe his tears. I tell him we won't leave his side and we will keep him safe.

As we drive, I dread watching him get poked again and sedated. I feel horrible not telling him about the poke but do not want to cause more anxiety. I look back at him, with his eye patch and new pirate rain coat. He stares at the rain smacking against the window.

When we arrive, we head straight to the surgery center. "Captain No Pants here for surgery!" Gavin says to the receptionist. She laughs and gives him a wristband with his name and birthdate. Gavin waits patiently to be called by the nurse.

In pre-op, Gavin picks out which hospital attire he will wear and is weighed. Steve helps him get dressed into the light blue pajamas, similar to the ones the nurse brought him the night he was first admitted. Gavin brought Hoppy with him, his blue bunny. The IV nurse stands at the door, and my stomach is in knots.

"Hello, I am here to help you with sedation," the nurse says as she enters his room.

"Hi," I reply, waiting for more information.

"We could do a mask which would help him fall asleep before getting an IV," she states.

"Gavin, do you want to try a mask or a poke to go to sleep?" I ask, wishing neither had to be an option.

"I don't want a poke but I'm scared of a mask that I won't be able to breathe," he says honestly.

She shows him the mask and lets him sniff different flavors that could be put into the mask, making it less scary. He picks out a Dr. Pepper® flavor, and Steve assures him he will be able to breathe.

Next, the two surgeons come in and explain the procedures. We are told Gavin may be sore on his tummy where the G-tube will be placed as well as the port site. Child Life distracts Gavin as we chat.

This time, Steve puts the surgical garb on and walks with Gavin to the OR. I kiss his forehead and tell him I will see him soon. I am sitting in the waiting room when Steve comes out of the surgery center. I pray, waiting for my baby to be in my arms again.

Nicole Pierson

THE SURGERIES ARE quick and went as well as expected. Gavin was moved from the operating room to the medical surgery recovery floor, unit 4200 of Children's Hospital in St. Paul. This part of the hospital is one of, if not the oldest, units in the hospital. The rooms are big enough to fit the bed, a small cart of supplies, a chair and the couch that was attached to the wall. If there are more than a couple people in the room at one time, it feels very confined.

This is much quieter than his first hospital stay. There were not doctors and therapists coming and going like a revolving door, or a stream of visitors nonstop. It was just Gavin, Steve and me, sitting in the quiet, small, but comfortable room. He had a few pain medications on board due to the surgeries and was sleeping most of the day.

I carefully peek under the covers at his bandages from surgery. His tummy and chest now have devices to help him during treatment. Two more scars freshly carved into his skin. It feels like we are doing more harm thus far. All we have done is inflict pain and not stop the mass in his brain from growing. As Gavin sleeps he looks very peaceful and innocent. His head is slightly tilted to the left, with his arms at his side. I am proud of him but also scared and incredibly sad. This is the first time since the beginning of all of this that it seems to be so real. Up to this point, there has always been so many people around and it almost felt like I was watching as an outsider, rather than living it myself.

I'm not sure why this moment is different and more real, but possibly because he is now equipped to start the journey of treatment. The shock is going away, and in place of it, is fear. A rollercoaster of emotions flow through me, and I am as devastated as I was the moment this began two weeks ago. Steve is sitting across the small room reading while I silently sob. Trying not to wake Gavin, I have my knees to my chest and let it all out. The room is dark, as clouds block the sun outside the shades of the windows. I feel empty and unsteady, the weight of what has transpired pushing down so heavily. I am not ready to watch Gavin go through this.

Silently I pray, "God, I cannot do this, how am I supposed to do this? Why Gavin?" I look up, suddenly frozen, as Gavin's hand reaches up for something.

Steve also looks up from his book as Gavin left his arm stretched out for a few seconds, and then gently put it down. Elbow first, his arm was placed back down next to his fragile body.

I get up quickly and walk over to the side of Gavin's bed without the IV pole and machines.

"Gavin, are you okay?" I ask concerned, tapping his shoulder. He doesn't move so I shake his arm a little and repeat myself, "Gavin, wake up!" with more worry in my tone. Steve is right next to me, ready to step in if needed. Is he okay?

He slowly opens his eyes, looking past me in the distance. Calmly he shifts to me as I continue.

"Gavin, what were you doing with your arm?"

He takes a slow, steady breath before telling me.

"Mom, I was trying to give God a hug, but YOU woke me up," he replies, with a bit of annoyance in his voice at the end. Chills cover my body instantly as his words set in. Steve looks at me, as if he needed reassurance about what he heard.

"You saw God?" I asked, slowly unpeeling the significance from what he said.

Nicole Pierson

"Yeah Mom, until you woke me up," he reminds me again. "Did He say anything to you?" I ask, wanting more details.

"No Mom, he didn't say any words, because he can talk to us without making a noise," he added. He was still pretty sleepy so I tucked him in and told him to rest. As I sat down in the chair again, I felt different. I felt so very small in a world so vast.

I sit without tears, still reeling about what I just saw and what Gavin told me. He has told me about his dreams before but never with such veracity. I wonder more, but know Gavin needs to sleep. Could this have really just happened? Did Gavin just imagine that it did? If so, why did the room feel so still? Back and forth, I wrangle with what I saw and what Gavin told me. Even though I saw this happen before my eyes, doubt begins to change that reality.

There have been times I have felt as if God intervened. There have been times it has happened to people I love. Why do I still doubt God? How can I both *feel* him and doubt his existence at the same time?

When my mom was a teenager, she worked at a diner in Minneapolis. A busy night left her leaving a few minutes late, just enough time to miss the last bus home. In a bad neighborhood, with no means of transportation or communication, she stood there in tears. All she could do was pray.

She told me that minutes later, a priest drove up and said to her, "God sent me. Let me bring you home." When I think about this story, I have been both in awe of the power of God, as well as doubtful about what the priest said. He may just feel that God sends him to help anyone in need, and saw my mom standing there alone. Did he truly mean, in the literal sense, that God sent him?

Gavin had been to church a few times. I wanted to get more involved with church but just did not feel connected to the church I had gone to since I was a child. It grew to be such a large congregation that I did not feel a part of it. Growing up in church, I sometimes felt like God was so real I could feel his presence, and at times wondered if He existed at all.

I know that Gavin's knowledge of God is limited and also that he is the most honest child I know. Too honest at times, when maybe he should have just fibbed a little bit. Like the time Grandma got him the wrong Spider-Man action figure and he told her so. He never meant to hurt anyone's feelings. And if he ever did, he felt terrible. He was just brutally honest and would even tell on himself. Like the time he and Grace put stickers all over my kitchen floor. He told me exactly what happened the second I walked in.

When I watched his arm reach out, I felt the room shift. It was not just what Gavin said, it was also how *I* felt. I was scared, yet comforted. I honestly thought something was wrong and maybe Gavin saw the light or something. Maybe, I had read about near death experiences too much, but that is why I woke him up. Then he tells me he was trying to give God a hug. I am back in the chair, watching Gavin sleep. The feelings I had right before seeing Gavin reaching out were full of fear and uncertainty.

What replaced them was calming, like when my mom would stroke my hair behind my ear and tell me not to worry. I felt as if I was being hugged and told that everything was going to be okay. If Steve had not been in the room too, I would have thought I imagined it, or that I heard Gavin

Nicole Pierson

wrong. But he was there, witnessing it as well. A non-believer, or at the very least a skeptic, saw it with his own eyes. There was no denying what we saw, or what Gavin told us. I vow to remember this moment, the shift of the room making me feel so comforted.

AFTER ONE NIGHT, Gavin was discharged. It felt good to have a short stay. We were hoping we would get out today because Gavin didn't want to miss his cousin Sam's birthday party. We carefully get Gavin into the van, and drive over to the party. Grace and Gage are there with my sister.

Steve drives carefully, so that Gavin does not shift much. His tummy is sore, and he is cautious of any movement near his G-tube. The tube comes out of his tummy, about two inches from his belly button. The tube was about eight inches long and was secured with medical tape to his tummy and tucked into his pants. The port was under his skin on the right side of his chest. It protruded out on his skinny body.

When we walk into the party, everyone is happy to see Gavin. He makes his way to the couch and slowly sits down, careful not to bump his G-tube. While there, he quietly watches everyone play around him. When they get near, he flinches, worried he will get bumped. We decide not to stay long, as we had to meet the home care nurse who would be teaching us how to use the pump for his G-tube and care for his new incisions.

Ha-lee was patient as she showed us how to use this new machine. She taught me how to do continuous feedings, and also how Gavin could wear a backpack with the pump inside of it. At this time, we were going to use it overnight to help get him nutrition as he begins chemo. I was thankful for her straightforward, caring personality.

GAVIN SOBS IN the living room with this arms wrapped around his legs and head down. I thought he was sad about everything that had happened.

I stop washing the table and walk over. "Gav, what's wrong?" I ask as I kneel by him.

He replies, "Mom I just miss God so much. He makes me feel calm and safe." I sit here in awe of this child, yearning to see God again.

"I know you miss Him but you know if you see Him again, you may not see Mom and Dad too, right?" I feared that God was going to take him and I wanted Gavin to want to stay with me. I was surprised when Gavin did not immediately tell me he would rather stay with us here on earth. It was frightening and oddly calming at the same time. For the rest of the day I wondered if God came to Gavin so he wouldn't be afraid to die.

Over the next few days, Gavin gave more details about that day in the hospital. As I fill the syringes with medicine, then pour some root beer, I hear Steve and the boys chatting in their room. Steve is putting a hook on Gavin's bottom bunk, to hang the tube from the feeding machine overnight.

I walk in to find Gage and Gavin sitting together. Gage is curious about what we are doing. Steve hooks Gavin up to the feeding tube and starts the machine as I give meds, not before it beeps several times and we figure out how to make it stop.

Without being prompted, Gavin says, "When I saw God, He was so bright and yellow. He brought his light down because my eyes couldn't see bright stuff," he continues. As he tells us this, he makes hand motions like he is pushing something down slowly. Steve and I look at each other afraid to say too much. Gavin hasn't really talked about this until now and he wants to share. As if he was our teacher, we listen intently to every word.

"So, He brought his light down. Wow. What did He look like, Gav?" I ask, sitting on his bed.

"He is very bright and God has curlers in his hair too, three on each side, like the ones we put in Grace's hair," he says with confidence. He tells us one thing after another, while we nod and listen.

"Remember how I told you God can talk to us without making a noise?" He keeps going without missing a beat.

"Yes Buddy, I remember that. Do you remember what God said to you?" I ask, not sure I want to know. What if God is taking my child?

"Yeah Mom, of course I do," he says calmly.

He pauses with a quick and gentle smile. "He told me, **Gavin, please be strong and brave.**"

We are speechless at this point. The way he described everything to us was in such detail, and so specific. Not like a dream where details are muddy. Everything he said was with conviction. It reminds me of someone who had an adventure and is now speaking about it passionately. He tells us that even though we saw that his eyes were closed, they were open. As he says this, his eyes are wide and alert.

Why would God visit Gavin? We are ordinary people. Thousands of children are fighting cancer. If God did give Gavin a message, what does it mean? We do not go to church as much as we should. It doesn't make sense. Aren't these God things supposed to happen to people like Jehovah's Witnesses who periodically show up at our door?

Last time they came, my dog nearly knocked them over as I struggled to keep my half-dressed children in the house. My hair wet from jumping out of the shower, and my breaths quick from running down the stairs, I tried to give them a few minutes of my time. Surely they would not view my family as people who would get a visit from God. We are not perfect—we are just us.

But we saw it. Every time I wonder why it happened, I tell myself that it did happen, regardless. I saw Gavin's arm reach up for something and watched as if it was set down beside him. It scared me. The room shifted. It felt full. My fear was replaced with warmth and comfort. I can't dismiss that feeling and I can feel it just as I can feel the air in my lungs. We kiss Gavin and tell him that he does need to be strong and brave. As we leave his room we are both quiet, not sure what to say.

We lie down and I turn to ask Steve, "Do you think God came to Gavin?" I have to know that he sees and hears what I do. He is the skeptic more so than me. Maybe I just want to believe all of this, maybe I am altering reality.

"It sure seems that way," he replies slowly as if in deep thought. That's it. No more is said as we fall asleep.

AS I SHARE about Gavin's visit on Caring Bridge, a few friends and family have called to share their knowledge of the Bible. They know I do not have it memorized. My grandma Elaine, who has always had a strong faith, reads a verse to me over the phone.

Nicole Pierson

"I looked, and there was a form that had the appearance of a man. From what seemed to be His waist down was fire, and from His waist up was something that looked bright, like the gleam of amber." Ezekiel 8:2.

The Bible story continues to discuss how the Lord stretched out his form of a hand. I turn to Gavin and ask him again, still on the phone with my grandma.

"Hey Gavin, can you tell me again what God looked like?"

He walks over and his eyes light up. "He was bright and yellow and he brought his light down," he says without looking up at me. He looks up at me and adds, "Oh, and he wore a robe. One that just is on one side, you know what I mean, Mom?" He continues playing with his dinosaurs as I stand there.

Every time I ask Gavin to repeat a detail, it is exactly the same. I decide to make a video asking him about it so I can share with family and friends. I want them to see the look in his eyes when he tells me what happened.

He sits in the unfinished basement, which we have made a play room. It is dark, because Gavin's eyes are very sensitive to light. The daylight comes through the patio door as I press record. "Okay Gavin, I was just wondering if you could tell me your story Buddy, about when you were in the hospital?"

Without hesitation, he begins.

"Um, well, I was at the hospital, and I was sleeping and I saw God when I was asleep. And he had like, these little things in his hair," he says while motioning his fingers by his head. In his blue pajamas, and black eye patch covering his left eye, he sits crisscross on the floor.

"He was all yellow, and," he pauses, shifting his eyes upward calmly. "I'm just so happy I got to see Him."

So far, his eyes have stayed focused on the TV next to me and he hasn't looked at the camera. I ask, "Did He say anything to you Gavin?"

He looks directly at me to answer, his eyes determined, "He said, Gavin, please be strong and brave."

As I continue asking questions, I pretend that I don't remember what he's already shared with me. I ask if God was next to him. "No, he wasn't next to me, he was just flying right in front of me," he holds both hands up in front of him while looking up.

"Wow, that's really cool. Did He say anything else to you?" I continue, still recording.

He turns his head, and puts his index finger to his mouth. Eyes squinted, as if trying to recall, he says, "No, not really. He just said, Gavin, please be strong and brave."

He tells me he saw a face, and that everything was yellow, but not too bright. "He brought His light down," he says. A few seconds later, he adds, "Hey, light and bright rhyme!"

When Gavin talks about what happened, he does not change character, or seem as if he is making it up. He is just five years old, telling us what happened. Whether he's rhyming words or describing God, he speaks and acts the same. I share the video to show this. I don't know what it means, or why Gavin had this experience, but to him, it is real.

"Is there anything else you want to say, Gavin?" I ask before stopping the recording.

"I love everybody that cares about me," he finishes.

Nicole Pierson

THE NEXT DAY, while walking out of Target with Gavin, I hear "Mrs. Pierson!" eagerly from a few feet away. I realize it is Abbey, a student of mine, and her mom, Melissa. Gavin sweetly chats with them for about ten minutes. He wanted to know about them and talk about anything and everything. After saying good bye, Melissa looks at me and says, "There is just something about him. He is an old soul." Everywhere we go, I keep hearing that. There is something about the way Gavin thinks, talks, does.

As we prepare for the next few months of treatment, I feel hope that all of this could mean something bigger than I can even comprehend. I wish that he was starting T-ball instead of starting chemotherapy, and that he could run and play without worry. I don't know if the treatment will do what it should, or if Gavin will be cured. This uncertainty sometimes makes it hard to breathe and keep moving forward. I remind myself that truly, none of us know the future. As we prepare for chemotherapy, I know that moving forward is our only option.

Gavin visiting his kindergarten class for an ice cream social.

Gavin recovering in the hospital with a visit from a therapy dog.

Nicole Pierson

Chapter Five

Trust in the Lord with all your heart
> and lean not on your understanding;
in all your ways submit to him,
> and he will make your paths straight.

Proverbs 3:5

As WE STARTED planning the first couple months of chemotherapy, it seemed manageable. Gavin will be in the hospital for three to five days for each round with three weeks off in between. They will be drawing labs weekly to be sure his white blood count and platelets are not too low.

When we were first in the hospital, I was given a binder, much like my three-ring binder for wedding planning or my Master's action research project. Except this binder was titled, "Family Handbook for Children with Cancer." Not as fun as planning a wedding, and I would rather do ten more action research projects than read it.

With every new piece of paper, the feeling that I was in a nightmare slowly went away. It was more real now. Every new piece of information takes us further away from the life we had. This was our life now, and coming to terms with that helped.

I had an urge to give the binder back. Accepting it seemed like accepting that my child had cancer. I still haven't been able to do that.

Everything I needed to know was in here, I thought reluctantly. I read every word, as if I was studying for a test. I quickly realize the wealth of information on the internet as well, which is good and bad. Google was my companion, along with many medical journals and websites. I wanted to know everything about his tumor, the treatments and side effects. I cannot change that he has a brain tumor, but I can be educated on what to expect from here on out.

We are learning how to clean Gavin's G-tube and flush it twice a day. It is time to clean it again. His tummy is still sore from surgery and he hates when it is touched.

"Gage, will you come sit by me?" Gavin asks.

At two years old, Gage looks up to his big brother. In his eyes, Gavin can run faster, climb higher, and jump farther. Gage walks over to Gavin without hesitation. He sits close and reaches out his hand. I cringe a little, hoping he doesn't pull the tube right out of Gavin's stomach.

Gavin squeezes Gage's hand as I touch his tummy with the cold alcohol wipe. I do it as quickly and softly as possible. As soon as it's over, Gage looks up at Gavin.

Nicole Pierson

"See Gavin, it not hurt," Gage says in a soft, reaffirming voice.

"Thanks, Bubba," Gavin replies.

Gage runs away and is back to playing. He didn't pull the tube out or get impatient while I cleaned Gavin's tummy. He stood there holding his hand and knew Gavin needed him. Once in a while, this journey offers amazing moments like this. Where time seems to stand still, and I am in awe. My life, that used to be even keel, now consists of agonizing lows and life-changing highs. I realize Grace and Gage will learn compassion on this journey, and they will make the world better because of it.

Gavin stays on the couch most of the day. He periodically asks me to bring his new pet turtle, Red, over to him. Steve found this little guy at the golf course recently and brought him home. After a few minutes, he wants to lay down again. It hurts his tummy to sit up.

As I PACK for chemo tomorrow, Gavin cries out in pain. Steve and I, coming from different floors, run into his room.

"My tummy hurts so bad!" Gavin cries.

As we look at it, the G-tube area is red and swollen, and his tummy is distended. I call Children's Hospital, and am told I need bring him in. As I hang up, I walk into Gavin's room.

"Sweetie, we are going to bring you to the hospital so you can feel better." I am trying to sound confident and not defeated. Gavin looks at me and doesn't say a word. He is miserable. Steve gets him dressed while I grab the clothes out of the dryer. As soon as I start walking down the stairs, I am sobbing. It comes on without warning. I am so frustrated, and angry. I am mastering the art of silent sobbing, as Grace and Gage come into the laundry room.

They both hug me, and Gage says, "Mommy, don't worry." I hug them tightly and tell them I love them and am sorry this is all happening. Grace tells me she is sad too, and that the guidance counselor had her fill out two slips with faces on them. One was the sad face, she tells me, and the other was the very sad face. I feel like I am in a tug of war. Gavin needs me, and Grace does too. She needs me to comfort her, and talk about her feelings. I stop crying and save it for another time. I don't have time to cry, or to help my seven-year-old cope with her feelings. I have to get to the ER, and it breaks my heart.

As I walk Grace and Gage to my parent's door, I kiss Grace on the cheek. She looks scared, so I tell her not to worry and that the doctors will help Gavin feel better. I pull my dad aside and let him know what she told me about the faces. He tells me he will talk with her. I pass the parenting torch for now.

After two hours at the ER, Gavin finally feels better. They had to perform an enema because with recent surgery and medications, he was constipated. It was critical to have this taken care of before beginning chemo. Gavin was given pain medication and we were soon on our way home. At nearly midnight, we picked our sleeping children up and placed them in their beds. Chemo was in eight hours. The emotional exhaustion of the night helped me fall asleep. For now, Gavin wasn't in pain and my babies were under one roof.

The double doors click and Dr. Petronio appears. He is smiling and directs us to the conference room. We tread with caution. Gavin has been in surgery for nine hours and we hope the tumor is gone.

Nicole Pierson

"I got all of it. I removed the whole tumor," he tells us with confidence.

I shake his hand and hug Steve. It's gone. The tumor is gone. Tears of happiness fill my eyes. I thank Dr. Petronio over and over.

Gavin lays in PICU as we wait for him to wake up. We share the news with everyone we know. The tumor is gone. It no longer occupies the center of my child's brain. Soon, Gavin can get back to life.

As I hold Gavin's hand I sing to him. He finally opens his eyes. They are moving together, and he says he can see better now. Double vision is gone. He says his incision is itchy but he is in no pain.

"Is the tumor gone?" Gavin asks.

"Yes Buddy, we got ALL of it. You won!" Steve tells him with excitement. A few days of recovery, and we will be home celebrating that the tumor is gone.

Gavin raises his arms up in a cheer and smiles.

I sit next to him watching TV as he rests, feeling the worry fall of my shoulders. He is going to be okay, I allow myself to think. We followed the map.

"Nikki! Wake up!" Steve says impatiently. It is 6:30 a.m., and we have to leave in thirty minutes. I have overslept. We are going to be late to chemo. As I sit up, I remember how it felt to hear those words, *I got all of it and removed the whole tumor.* Motivation. Let's start shrinking this tumor so we can get back to life.

We manage to get the kids dressed and into the minivan in about thirty-five minutes. Not bad. By 7:10 a.m., we have dropped Grace and Gage off at daycare and are on our way to Minneapolis. If traffic isn't too bad, we should make it there on time.

Although Gavin's first two hospital stays were in St. Paul, his chemotherapy will be in Minneapolis. The

Hematology/Oncology clinic is also at the Minneapolis campus, and that is where Gavin will be going for his weekly labs. Knowing we will be here a few days, we packed activities, movies, and extra clothes. Steve is working, so I will be staying with Gavin and he will be home with Grace and Gage. Not knowing what to expect, I asked Steve to come with us the first day.

WALKING OFF THE elevator onto the seventh floor of the hospital was like walking into another world. It was a world we are now a part of. As we enter the unit, all eyes were on us. I figure they must know that Gavin is the new kid on the block. Not really a neighborhood I thought we would ever live in, but we were the newly diagnosed, recently heartbroken, seventh floor occupants.

I look around and realize how many other children are fighting for their lives, too. I am not sure why, but I thought there would just be a few. Cancer in children is not as rare as I once thought. Gavin, with the exception of a small shaved area from surgery, still has his light blonde hair and good color to his skin. Most of the kids were unfortunately seasoned. They had all the marks of chemo. Thin bodies, pale skin and no hair. Machines are their companion.

A girl about thirteen, smiles at Gavin and he waves back as we walk past. She has a beautiful knitted cap to cover her bald head. I think of girls her age, who care more about their hair than their homework. Here, this girl is just smiling and making friends with new chemo patients. I suppose she doesn't have to worry about having a bad hair day like her peers. But she also doesn't get to be at school, or go to the dance, or be in the school play. God, this isn't fair.

Nicole Pierson

I cannot believe Gavin is walking these halls and will soon have all of the equipment too. I try to focus ahead and ignore my emotions. Surely I had seen a child with cancer before. Why does this feel so different?

I think about the times I had—on Lifetime movies, or St. Jude's commercials. But in real life? Not that I can recall. Now that I was with children who had real lives before their diagnosis as Gavin did, I was, for the first time, truly seeing them. I was just as sad as I had been when I watched those movies, but this was different.

I am seeing Gavin's future, and it fills me with anger and fear. How can this really be the life for these kids? They should be outside playing in the warm spring weather, not filling the halls of the seventh floor. With each step, I am trying not to notice the suffering. After all, I cannot just cry it out on the couch, and flip the channel to something happier like I did before.

This is real. This is our life.

We make it to our room which we will have for the next three days. It was impressively large. There is a nice bathroom with a shower, large couch that folds out to a bed, and a lot of space around the bed. There is a nice flat screen TV, which is the first thing Gavin notices.

"Wow! Look at the size of my TV! This is awesome, like a hotel!" he exclaims.

As Steve and Gavin start unpacking some of Gavin's things, I talk with the nurse. She explains what IV medications he will get along with chemo. They will be giving him anti-nausea medication and fluids to constantly flush out the chemo.

Gavin gets comfortable in his bed as the nurse puts Emla numbing cream on his chest, where she will access his port. She covers it with a clear bandage, and he puts his shirt back on, which reads, "Love Root Beer, Hate Cancer." We thought it was perfect for his first day of chemo.

"I'll be back in about twenty minutes," the nurse says as she walks out of the room.

"Mom and Dad, they have movies on the TV! Can I watch one?"

We flip through the menu and I am happy to see there are some for parents too. I am sure I will be watching those when I can't sleep. *The Lorax* begins, and Gavin is lost in Thneedville as the nurse prepares to access his port. She counts as Gavin holds my hand. One, two, three and it's done. Thankfully, it is much easier than placing an IV.

After initial fluids, I watch as Gavin is prepped for chemo. Another nurse comes in with the chemo bag. She is dressed in a gown, hat, and mask. To protect her from the harsh chemical composition of the chemotherapy drugs, the nurse cannot risk touching a drip of it, yet it will flow through Gavin. My stomach turns in angst. But it will shrink the tumor, I convince myself. I have to stay focused on better days. I remember my dream. It *has* to come true.

If things were not real yet, they were now, as chemo begins to pump into his veins. I pray we are beginning to kill this monster. I pray it doesn't damage the rest of his body in the process.

I watch him like a hawk for the first twenty minutes. I was scared. I thought maybe he would start violently vomiting or that the poison would cause him immediate pain. But he is acting fine, and continues to watch *The Lorax*, as if chemo was

Nicole Pierson

an every-day occurrence. I decide that every time I look at the chemo bag, I will imagine it destroying cells that are trying to destroy Gavin.

Chemo is the lesser of two evils.

As the movie nears the end, Steve leaves to pick up the kids from school. "Be strong Bud," he says to Gavin, kissing him on the forehead. "I will Dad," Gavin replies.

I begin to look through the welcome folder. We may as well get comfortable. "Oh, Gavin, there is Bingo and you can win prizes—do you want to try it tomorrow? Or, we can do a craft in the playroom." I tell him so he can consider his options.

Neither of these pique his interest. I see there is a channel with programs specifically for kids at Children's, and flip to it. He's watching. Children's Hospitals do a terrific job of making horrible situations more tolerable. Despite the fact that all children on the newly remodeled Hematology Oncology floor were there because they needed chemo, there were smiles. They had daily activities, a play room, scooters, PAC-MAN and Gavin's favorite—*The Dude*.

The Dude was awesome. Each day his show played for kids at both St. Paul and Minneapolis hospitals. He performs the show live from a studio in Minneapolis. During one of his shows, Gavin called in to answer a trivia question. He acted as if Gavin was the coolest person on this earth, asking if he could meet him and get his autograph after the show. Gavin's face lit up with excitement when he walked in an hour later. In the flesh!

He makes the kids smile and forget. They forget that their toes are numb, their hair is gone, and that without a constant drip of Zofran they would be puking all day. He helps them forget all they are missing while they fight for the chance to grow up.

With Gavin's first day of chemo complete, I make the couch as comfortable as I can and try to fall asleep. I find comfort knowing that finally, we have begun to attack the tumor inside of Gavin's precious head.

Finally, we are on the offensive side of this battle.

Chapter Six

If we believe that tomorrow will be better,
we can bear a hardship today.

Thich Nhat Hanh

GAVIN DID NOT get sick today, despite the nurses telling him he might. He kept ordering ham and cheese sandwiches, and managed to keep them down. It is our third day here, and if all goes well, he will be discharged later this afternoon.

We had some visitors the second day and Gavin decided to play Bingo. We also went for a short walk to the playroom and played basketball and PAC-MAN. He slept a lot after that. When he slept, I researched and read, and slept sometimes too. It has been uneventful and boring, which I am taking as a win.

During the past two nights, Gavin woke up often having to use a urinal. When chemo is pumped, so are lots of fluids, which makes for a constantly full bladder. He would press the nurse button, but usually I got to him first.

After Gavin has breakfast—his favorite, pancakes and sausage—Steve calls to see what time we need to be picked up. He also tells me that Dylan, my brother, found three more tiny painted turtles just like Red! Gavin is ecstatic about coming home to his new pets. As the last few drips of chemo pump through his body, he thinks about what he will name them.

"I am going to let Grace name one of them," he says.

He decides he will name one of them Trooper, after himself, and the other one Norman, after dad's childhood pet turtle. When the nurse comes in, he tells her all about it. She shows me how to do the injections at home and puts a small catheter in his arm. The injections are full of a medicine which stimulates growth of healthy cells. I sign discharge papers and Steve meets us to help carry everything. I walk out feeling like we can do this. Chemo is not so scary after all.

AS SOON AS we get home, Gavin goes to the turtles. They help distract him and make him happy. Grace decided on a name for the third turtle. Our four turtles were officially named Red, Trooper, Norman and Emily. Emily happens to be Grace's middle name.

The next few weeks we plan our lives around Gavin. A Twins game, walks, and turtle races were some of the things he could do. Gavin's kindergarten class invited him to school and presented an iPad for him they had raised funds to purchase. It was really nice to visit and for Gavin to see that his friends at school cared. They sat in the grass and ate ice cream.

My hope, as I watch them, is Gavin will kick this tumor's butt over the summer and be running with them next fall. Maybe they will come back with stories of camping trips and fishing, and Gavin can tell them he beat his brain tumor. I naively thought, *a day will come when all of our new worries will dissipate and we will go back to our old life.* I needed to believe this.

We had two clinic appointments before the next round of chemo. At these appointments, Gavin had his port accessed and blood drawn. The clinic always made blood draws as pain free as possible. The numbing cream helped the sting of the poke and after blood was taken, kids could send it in the rocket ship to the lab. Most visits we brought Gage, who was nearly three. He would sometimes get to press the button and send the rocket ship.

Every step of the way, Gavin wants to know why we are doing what we are doing. He understands that the medicine needed to shrink the tumor can change his blood, which is why he has to be poked every week.

Gavin never wants things to be sugar coated. When nurses explain the blood pressure cuff as an arm hug, he would just look at them matter-of-factly and say, "You mean blood pressure? Yeah, I know and I don't think it's like a hug at all." He was fighting for his life, and he knew it. Unlike most kids who were about to turn six, he understood, and was wise beyond his years.

THE SECOND ROUND of chemo was not as nice to Gavin. It proved to be stronger despite nonstop Zofran, and Gavin got very sick. It was five days rather than three. He didn't participate in as many activities. He wanted to lay in bed to watch movies.

"Mom, I am going to be sick!" he shouts, just seconds before puking. I got up as quickly as I could but it was too late. I rub his back while he continues to vomit all over himself and the bed, while simultaneously pressing the nurse call button.

"Mom, hurling is not my favorite thing to do," he says when he is done.

"I know Buddy, I'm sorry," I try.

The nurse helps us get Gavin up without tangling all of the lines, and cleans his bed. I wash Gavin and dress him into clean pajamas. *This is shrinking the tumor*—I think to myself each time he is sick again.

I hear Grace and Gage paddling down the hallway and turn to Gavin. I smile at him and look towards the door, letting him know he has visitors. "Bubba! Grace!" he says as they walk in.

"Hey, Gavin," Grace says as she sits next to him. They bring energy to the room that only kids can. Gage is eating Cheetos while the poison of the day pumps into Gavin's veins. At least we are all together, even if it does have to be at Children's Hospital. I look over, and realize that a Cheeto is stuck, and Gage is choking. The nurse, who was checking on Gavin, looks at me as I pat Gage's back. I keep thinking it will go down. It hasn't though, and he is now panicking. Code Blue was called as the nurse and I try to help him. It seems as if it has been minutes but probably was about thirty seconds. My heart is pounding as about ten nurses show up at the door, and he finally takes a breath. The nurse cancels the Code Blue and I try to slow my racing heart.

The only other time one of my children was choking happened to be Gavin, at about the same age. We were at a neighborhood birthday party when all of a sudden he came up to me, tugging at my shirt. When I looked down, he was not breathing. I didn't know what to do and yelled, "He's choking!" A nurse happened to be there and started working on Gavin. Still, he was not breathing, and someone began to dial 911. Finally, a piece of candy came out and he was crying. A beautiful cry. No more Cheetos, Gage. No more Code Blues. I can only handle one crisis at a time.

After they left, a radiation oncologist came to chat with me about possible radiation. This would happen after chemo and surgery. She seemed to have a goal of scaring me.

"Side effects can include memory loss, thyroid damage, organ damage, lower IQ," she begins to tell me. I heard every single one, but had made a promise to myself I would not think too far in advance. We are still dealing with chemo side effects right now, and radiation is far down the road on our map. I calmly listen to the side effects, legs crossed and nodding. I must not have been giving her the worried response she expected, apparent by her sudden change of tone and acceleration of her piercing words.

"You do realize it could be really bad. Like he may feel so hungry that you will have to lock cupboards and possibly restrain him to his bed during the night so he doesn't sneak food," she tells me lacking even one ounce of compassion.

"Okay," I reply slowly, stunned at how she was acting. I wonder what the purpose of this visit was. I could have read about the side effects in my binder. Did she want to worry me? As if I have a damn choice in the matter? I am growing quite angry.

If Gavin's doctor says he needs radiation, we will do it and hope for the best. This woman, with her high heels and perfect makeup, doesn't get it. She does not understand my calm demeanor is my defense mechanism. I refuse to worry about things that are not happening right now. I heard the scary side effects and I know how bad they are. I want to tell her to leave and go ruin some other person's day. Bedside manner is not one of her strengths.

"Do you have any questions?" she says before leaving.

"Nope, I think you pretty much covered every horrible scenario there is," I reply bitingly. Thank God that's over.

After five long days, and not much activity, Gavin was discharged. At home, we distracted Gavin with his turtles, and his birthday wish list. He was going to be six soon and we were going to celebrate. When the weather was nice, we even got Gavin outside for a lemonade stand and a careful run through the sprinkler, with his tummy and chest covered of course.

One warm day, we went to the Como zoo in St. Paul, which was one of Gavin's favorite places. The tigers are usually hard to spot, and if found, they seem to sleep. Today, as we walked past, one walked right up to the glass. Gavin's eyes met with the tiger's and the tiger didn't move.

"Mom, look at the tiger! He is staring right at me!" Gavin shouted.

He sat there for about five minutes, just staring into this tiger's eyes. There was something about this moment. Gavin was matching the eye of the tiger, its determination and strength. What was so crazy about it, is that the tiger stared at Gavin just as long, as if he knew Gavin's battle. They had a connection, a shared look of courage. Gavin knew he had a brain tumor, but he was not going to fear it. Just as a tiger stares down his prey, with the confidence that he will win, Gavin will fight without fear. I snapped a picture of them

Nicole Pierson

staring into each other's eyes, as if frozen that way while people buzz around them.

I KNEW WHAT to expect for side effects but I didn't think they would begin so quickly. As Gavin sat in the bath, the poison began to show its power. There are moments when reality feels like a punch in the face. Moments like this, that can't be ignored or dealt with later.

As I run my fingers through Gavin's hair, I feel some of it come out into my hands. I look and suddenly have a handful of beautiful blonde hair. My heart sinks.

"Mom, what is it?" Gav asks, knowing my expression has changed.

I stare at it, as if I don't know what it is. I am having trouble processing. I withdraw from what just happened and manage to answer him.

"Oh just a little hair, no big deal," I say reassuringly. It really is, just hair. But it signifies so much more than that.

I tell Gavin I will be right back and walk away with his hair in my hand. The hair that was just attached to his precious head. I sit on my bed, and recall his first haircut. I took some of his hair home with me in a baggie. He was one. It was like a rite of passage, getting your child's first haircut and saving a lock of curls.

This was a different rite of passage. Not one that I want to put in a scrapbook. My baby was losing his hair because he is going through chemo and has a brain tumor! I am crying now, without remembering when the tears began. I wonder if they will ever stop! Steve finds me and doesn't need to ask what is wrong. All I can do is sit here staring at his hair glistening in my hand. I feel numb. How will I do this? How will I watch my child go through hell?

Steve gently pats my back and goes into the bathroom to help Gavin rinse the rest of the shampoo. He then shaves Gavin's head, just as he did to his own head ten years before. As I listen to the vibration hug Gavin's head so tightly, I feel defeated. I had hoped he could still have his hair a while longer, maybe until his sixth birthday. I hope if chemotherapy is strong enough to take his beautiful blonde hair, it is strong enough to shrink the tumor.

There is a cycle of emotions that play out almost daily. Despair, Anger, Fear, Hope. Rinse, and Repeat. While Steve finishes shaving his head, at least we are ahead of the monster's next move. If only we knew what the move following this one was going to be.

GAVIN IS GETTING excited for his *Avengers* birthday party. Family and friends join us and celebrate Gavin turning six and Gage about to turn three. Their birthdays are only three weeks apart, so, we decided with everything going on, we would have one big party for them.

Gavin wore a fedora hat to cover his bald head, and an eye patch so he wouldn't see double. He smiled for the camera and enjoyed each present. He was happy to be home, as he could still be in the hospital.

Two days ago, while at a routine checkup, he was diagnosed with shingles. His medical team, realizing it was his birthday, allowed him to go home on IV antibiotics. We left his port accessed and I administered Acyclovir at home. Shingles, chemo side effects, and double vision, but he was happy.

Nicole Pierson

THE THIRD ROUND of chemo was supposed to be easy like the first. It was the same regimen and was only three days rather than five. This marks the half way point of the six rounds of chemo, getting us closer to a cure. So far, this stay has mimicked the first and has been easier on Gavin. It is our last day, and after the poison is done today, we get to go home. However, I begin to notice some new symptoms and point them out to his nurse.

"When he sleeps, he leans to the right and ends up turned all around," I explain. Last night, he was constantly turning until he was upside down.

"Also, when he is watching TV, his head will fall to the right and I have to constantly adjust it for him," I continue. I assure her this is new.

"Hmmm, well, I can let the doctor know and see what he wants to do," she assures me.

About ten minutes later, the doctor knocks and I invite him in. I explain to him what I told the nurse. I also mention Gavin's pupils are different sizes. All of the small things I had kept a mental note of, seemed to point to something. He agreed these were concerning and decided to order an MRI. Gavin already had his port accessed, so we decide to sedate him for the scan. I visit with my friend Emmie, and cousin Donna as he sleeps.

I am anxious and scared. What is causing these new symptoms? I feel like I know something is terribly wrong, but keep reminding myself not to jump to conclusions. Gavin is wheeled back to his room and is slowly waking up. After some juice and crackers, I get to take him home.

"You will get a call tomorrow about the scan results," the nurse tells me as she hands me his discharge papers.

I carefully put Gavin in the van, propping his head with a pillow because he was still a little groggy. He slept, while my mind raced. We have been poisoning this tumor for two months, what could possibly be causing these new symptoms?

At almost 10:00 p.m., we pull into the driveway. I texted Steve to come out and help us get inside. He carried Gavin to his bed while I grabbed our bags.

As I begin to unpack, my phone rings. The caller ID shows a blocked number. I instantly know it is oncology. They don't make calls this late unless it is bad.

"Hello?" I say cautiously.

"This is Dr. Schultz." Her voice says it all.

My throat closes as I sit down at the computer desk. Steve looks at me and knows it is serious. I cannot believe what I am hearing.

"The tumor has grown, significantly."

Steve hears the concern in my voice and waits to hear what words were just spoken. I quietly mouth to him, "It grew." He sits down on the stairs as I finish the conversation.

I hang up, speechless. Steve and I look at each other with nothing to say. I walk over to him and sit down to cry. Trying to be quiet I say, "Chemo was supposed to shrink it, and now it's bigger." We go back and forth, trying to comprehend how this happened.

This tumor—we poisoned it, how can it have grown? What if it has spread?

Oh my God, what if Gavin is dying? I cannot lose him! "God, please do not take him from me!" I plead.

Nicole Pierson

Gavin and the tiger at Como zoo. May 2012.

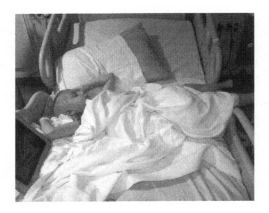

Completely turning upside down, the night before the scan,
June 2012.

Chapter Seven

Do not be anxious about anything,
but in every situation, by prayer and petition,
with thanksgiving, present your requests to God.

Philippians 6

A BULLY DOESN'T play fair. A bully waits until you are
vulnerable and unable to defend yourself. A bully tries to take
the life of a six-year-old child. Anxiety about what this growth
means has me reminding myself to breathe. We had a plan and
now I feel so lost. The only moments I am able to feel peace
is when I imagine God coming down to Gavin. I repeat His
words. Be strong and brave.

After little sleep, we are up and headed to the clinic. I
need to see how big this monster is, and discuss what we are
going to do to destroy it. A feeling of emptiness washes over
me as I stare out the passenger window. If poison cannot kill
this tumor, what can? The thought is paralyzing.

Keep it together, I think, as we pull into the parking
ramp of Minneapolis Children's Hospital.

Nicole Pierson

On our way in, we walk past a little boy about Gavin's age who is sitting on a bench with his mom. Gavin notices he has a cast on his left arm, and looks up to me with concern.

"Mom, I feel so bad for that kid. He has a broken arm," he says quietly as we pass by.

"Oh that is sweet Buddy, but it looks like he gets to go home and I am sure it will heal." My reassuring smile masks my broken heart. I wish that was all we were here for. Gavin's compassion for others amazes me. He has a monster taking over his brain, and he cares that this boy broke his arm. God thank you for giving me this child, I think as we wait for the elevator.

If not a broken arm, I will take a brain tumor that follows the rules. Last night, we had to tell Gavin his tumor grew. He didn't get angry, or cry, or ask us why he had to do chemo for nothing. Rather, he thought a moment before speaking and said, "Dad and Mom—I want to call my tumor Joe Bully."

"Okay, why is that?" I asked as I kneeled down next to him.

"Well, because I don't like bullies, and he is a bully," he told us.

"And because Dr. Petronio's name is Joe. It will be a battle, and I think my Joe is stronger," he continued with confidence.

As WE WAIT in the Hematology/Oncology Clinic, Gavin heads over to play PAC-MAN with Steve. I usually play with him before appointments but today, I can't. Getting myself up and dressed was quite the task, and walking feels like swimming upstream against a powerful current.

Be Strong and Brave

As I watch the other children come in and out around me, fighting for their lives too, I feel like shouting, "HELP US!" I share a few half smiles with other moms like me. It is an unspoken word of encouragement. None of us planned to be sitting in an oncology clinic. We dreamt of sitting on the sidelines while our children played baseball, or danced on stage. We dreamed of them growing up. As we all sit here, trying to be positive, we all know. We know that inside, we are trying to keep it together. Each of us wishing we could protect our children from cancer.

I replay everything Gavin has been through since being diagnosed. My mind tries to piece together why God visited Gavin, why the tumor grew, and why any of this is happening.

"*Am I losing him, God?*" *I demand an answer. Is that why you visited Gavin, so he wouldn't be scared when you take him home? Please don't take my baby, please let him stay.*"

I did not just allow poison through my child's veins for nothing, did I? I am so scared and feel vulnerable, unknowing of what this appointment will turn out to be. I was strong until last night, when we were all putting one foot in front of the other. Now, it seems we have taken a giant leap backwards. The path just got longer and I'm not even sure if we are on it anymore.

We meet with Linda from Oncology, who shows us the MRI images from last night. I hesitantly walk to the screen and see it is much bigger. It pushes Gavin's brain out of its way, uncaring about the effects of doing so. It is relentless. No doubt, it is a bully.

"So, now what do we do?" I ask as tears fall off my cheeks. Usually, I can keep it together but since last night I cannot stop. When the needle pierces Gavin's chest, or when he's being sedated again, I go somewhere else. I have learned it hurts too much to be fully present at those times. If I don't withdraw, I am giving fear too much of myself. I stay strong for Gavin. Today is different and it is impossible to keep it in anymore. Linda sees my pain, as she has seen on the faces of mothers before me. She hears the desperation in my voice.

"This changes the plan, but it does not necessarily change the outcome," she replies.

She encourages Gavin to punch Joe Bully on the screen. He makes a fist and punches at the image of his enemy. His fist and Joe Bully match closely in size, a sickening thought. It is ugly, now with more cysts than the last time I saw it just eight weeks ago. Gavin gets labs drawn to check tumor markers, which will tell us if what has grown is benign, or cancerous. He sends his blood through the rocket ship and we are on our way home.

Before we leave, we stop at the reception desk to set up an appointment with Dr. Petronio, the surgeon who did Gavin's biopsy. We will be discussing the possibility of surgery in a couple of days. Until then, I will cling to the little hope I have. The hope that we can still win. At home I go through the motions until we can speak to the neurosurgeon.

AFTER DROPPING THE kids off at daycare, I realize I am nearly out of gas. The neurosurgery clinic called me this morning, and asked me to come an hour early, or reschedule for later this week. There is no way I am going to wait to hear what the surgeon thinks. I cannot go through more days of not knowing Gavin's options. So as fast as we could, we got out the door.

Be Strong and Brave

As I pull up to pump gas, I swipe my card and plan to put just enough gas in to get us there. St. Paul is about forty minutes away, and I have thirty-five minutes to get there. It won't read my card after a few attempts, so I run in impatiently. There is a guy in front of me buying lottery tickets and cigarettes. He is taking forever! I want to scream at him for taking so long. If only my life was so simple, I think as I wait. If only I had time.

After finally getting gas, I am hurrying to get to the clinic. A few minutes late, we walk as fast as we can to the elevators. Luckily, Dr. Petronio's clinic is to the left as soon as we get onto the third floor. Gavin goes through the little door, made just for kids, and I meet him on the other side.

Gavin's vitals are checked, and we now wait for the doctors. Today we will see the oncologist and the neurosurgeon. Since Gavin's diagnosis, I have always felt better when these two are near. I hope today is the same. Gavin sits quietly on the edge of the bed, with his head down as if in reflection of some sort. Last night, we told him that although Joe Bully grew, hopefully the chemo killed the cancer cells. He shrugged his shoulders and said, "Okay." He usually has more to say. I think he feels defeated but is afraid to tell me. He hates to see me sad. The few tears I have shed in his presence usually end quickly because he catches them. As I watch him, I know he hurts.

I silently pray, "God, please be with Gavin. You told him to be strong and brave. He needs you if he's going to do this. Amen."

Gavin calmly swings his legs back and forth and stares at the ground. "I really didn't want to have a brain tumor," he says to me in a soft voice.

Nicole Pierson

"I know Gav. I don't want you to have a brain tumor either. Joe Bully is about to meet his match though," I assure him.

"Come in," I say as the door slowly opens. Dr. Schultz and Dr. Petronio walk in together. They pull up the images once again, and this time I just stay back. I've seen enough and don't need to see it again. That monster is etched into my memory.

"Well, it certainly is bigger, and it is pushing on the left side of his brain," Dr. Petronio concludes. He does a neurological exam and explains that Gavin has developed some right-sided weakness. This is why he kept leaning to the right. I learn that the tumor is now pressing on critical areas more than before. These areas include the brain stem, cerebral veins, the temporal lobe, and other places I cannot pronounce. It is serious, and the pressure needs to be dealt with. Surgery is scheduled for next week.

"He's a really sweet boy, isn't he?" Dr. Petronio says as he examines Gavin and checks his reflexes. I tell Dr. Petronio how strong Gavin has been and that he has named his tumor Joe Bully. "I've never had anyone name their tumor before," he says with a smile. Gavin shrugs his shoulders, and smirks.

"Which Joe do you think will win?" he asks Gavin.

"I'm betting on you Dr. Petronio," Gavin says confidently.

Dr. Schultz asks us to wait in the lobby for a few minutes so she can get the results of the tumor markers. These were elevated at diagnosis, which told us cancer was present. Minutes feel like hours. My palms sweat as I continue to check the time on my phone. Only four minutes have passed.

A smiling face appears and I know instantly.

The cancer is gone!

"The tumor markers are normal!" Dr. Schultz says in a hopeful and positive tone. We hug and celebrate. It is the good news within the bad. We have a bigger tumor, but thankfully what is left, is likely all benign. A moment of relief washes over me. The chemo wasn't for nothing. But why did it grow?

Growing Teratoma Syndrome (GTS). This is Gavin's updated diagnosis. There are theories about why it grew during chemotherapy. In mixed tumors, chemo can kill cancerous cells, allowing benign cells to grow rapidly. There is some research for new treatments, and Dr. Schultz assures me she will be looking into it. We decide that after surgery, we will discuss what's next.

"Bye Dr. Schultz," Gavin says sweetly.

"Bye Buddy, I'm cheering you on!" she replies.

As I hold Gavin's hand on our way out of the clinic, I can feel him leaning into me. It is a reminder of how fast the tumor is growing. I feel that with every step, another cell is duplicated. I imagine it growing uncontrollably and wish we could do surgery now. He walks guarded and unsteady as we try to remember where we parked. Once I unlock the door, I help him carefully into his booster seat and kiss his forehead.

I walk around the van and take a purposeful deep breath. "We are going to fight, and we will never give up," I say as I start the car. I put my sunglasses on, telling Gavin it is so bright outside. A good way to hide my swollen, glossy eyes. We may have leaped backwards, but we are on a new path, I reflect as I hop onto I-94 West towards home.

Nicole Pierson

Joe Bully was chasing after Gavin's life, and we are running as fast as we can.

IT'S FATHER'S DAY and we are trying not to think about the elephant in the room, as we have a barbeque at my sister's. Brain surgery is in a few days. Gavin is more tired than usual, so he cuddles up with Steve on a big chair and takes a nap. I attempt to smile as I watch my other children play in the yard. The image of Joe Bully keeps flooding my mind. It was a golf ball when we first saw it, and now it is a peach. A peach, in a six year-old's brain! We need to get it out. I think about what Dr. Petronio said when it was the size of a golf ball. He told us it was bigger than he would like it to be. He had hoped it would shrink to half the size before attempting to remove it. Instead, it doubled. My plate of food sits on the table, untouched. I join conversations just enough to look present, but I am not here. I replay the heartbreak of this morning when Gavin was making a card for Grandpa.

"Mom, I need some help writing," Gavin said as he picked up a pencil. He folded a red card for Grandpa and wanted to write the words 'I love you'.

"Okay, Gav, I will just help you move the pencil," I said, knowing he could write last week, although it was getting a little shaky.

I put my hand over his to guide him. When we were ready to sign his name, he told me he could do it himself, so I took my hand away. He could barely grip the pencil. After the first letter, he stopped as tears filled his eyes.

"Mom, I just really want to write my name for Grandpa, and I can't," he cried.

Be Strong and Brave

"It's okay, Gav. I will help you finish. Joe Bully is trying to mess with you, that's all. But you are stronger, and one day your handwriting will be perfect again." Moms have to pretend they know sometimes. I don't know if he will write again, or if he will lose more abilities. I don't know if he will win.

I head to the bathroom so I can cry out the pain. It's not that my family wouldn't support me if I decided to stay and cry. I just have to allow myself to release the built up emotions, and doing so privately helps me move on and stay strong for Gavin.

AROUND 2:00 A.M., my nightly routine of research is complete, and I know I need sleep. My eyes are shutting as I turn off the lamp and my laptop. I have learned that Growing Teratoma Syndrome has one treatment that is curative.

Surgical removal of the entire tumor.

If it cannot be fully removed, it will keep growing back and is considered unresectable. I find a few articles about new treatments, but the overall synthesis of my research tonight is that we have to remove the tumor completely. If we can't, there are limited treatments and no cure. Every case of unresectable teratoma I read about, resulted in death, owing to the progression of the disease.

Sitting next to Gavin, I hear him gasp for air a few times. It worries me enough to wake Steve. He listens to Gavin's breathing and hears the gasps too. Knowing the tumor is pressing on many critical structures, it did not take us long to decide we were going to the ER.

There is no traffic in the middle of the night, so we get to Minneapolis in about twenty minutes. Our other children are once again at my parents. Thankfully they live less than a mile away. I tell the nurse he is having difficulty breathing and he is scheduled to have surgery in a few days for his brain tumor. She brings him back right away.

Note to self: Say the words "brain tumor" and "difficulty breathing" and you bypass all of the paperwork.

Note to self: This is serious.

His oxygen saturations are at 87%, when they should be between 97 and 100. He clearly is not getting enough oxygen. The reason why is not so clear. His hemoglobin has been low since his last chemo, which could cause shortness of breath. Coinciding with that, the tumor is pressing on his brain stem which controls breathing, which, is really important.

Thankfully, the nurse understands that and quickly gives Gavin oxygen. We are not leaving anytime soon—I think as the cannula for oxygen is placed into his nostrils. Oncology was paged, so we now wait for a plan.

Gavin falls asleep around 4:00 a.m. His chest is rising and falling more easily, and with oxygen, his saturations are normal. I push my chair close to his bedside and share his pillow. I think I have about a fourth of it, but it's enough.

Just as I doze off, the ER doctor walks in. Look alert, I tell myself. Pure exhaustion makes this difficult. He tells us Gavin will be admitted tonight and be given oxygen and fluids. In the morning, Oncology will check his counts and decide if he needs a blood transfusion. I was extremely tired, and couldn't think of any questions. I knew this was serious but my body demanded rest, and for now, I knew my baby could breathe. I knew we were in good hands at Children's, and that it was going to be a long day tomorrow. We made our way to the seventh floor and slept a few more hours.

Be Strong and Brave

DR. SCHULTZ WALKS into Gavin's room around 9:00 a.m. to tell us Gavin needs a blood transfusion, as his hemoglobin has continued to drop. It's decided he will have the transfusion in Minneapolis, and she will coordinate with Neurosurgery about surgery. For the next few hours, I watch as someone's blood pumps into Gavin's veins. The seriousness of his situation sinking in further.

A blood transfusion, difficulty breathing, and loss of motor functions. This has all happened in the past week. As much as I don't want brain surgery, I am afraid of the alternative. This bully isn't going to stop invading Gavin's brain, and what could happen next?

We are watching *Spy Kids* for about the twentieth time in the past eight weeks. Gavin loves going somewhere else besides his hospital room, and engaging in movies to escape his own reality. It helped him forget, and didn't require much effort or energy.

The blood transfusion is now complete, and Dr. Schultz comes back with a plan. "With neurosurgery in three days, we want to keep Gavin monitored. His color looks better with the transfusion, but the tumor is also pressing on his brain stem. We will transfer him to St. Paul until surgery," she says carefully, making sure we understand the plan. We begin to prepare for a trip over to St. Paul. Gavin is excited to go there.

He hopes to see nurse Travis. I am thankful for Travis. Because of him, Gavin isn't sad he has to spend three extra nights in a hospital. He forgets about the transfusion he just had, or the struggle to take a breath. He forgets that in three

Nicole Pierson

days, a part of his skull will be removed, meaning, he will have a craniotomy.

IN ST. PAUL'S intensive care unit, I watch the machines that tell me every heartbeat and breath. I am glued to them at all times, alerting the nurses when I think something is wrong. The tumor grew so fast, and I worry about the damage it is doing every second we do nothing.

Our days are boring, something the intensive care unit is totally okay with. Visitors help the time go by, and Gavin did get to see nurse Travis. Tonight Gavin is getting Cheerios put on his head. Really, they are fiducial markers which are used for mapping during surgery. Gavin is not a fan. They have to use glue and hold them on his head.

"Be careful of my scars," Gavin says to the technician. After about ten minutes, he has a head of cheerios and is ready for brain surgery.

"Tomorrow I have surgery?" Gavin asks.

"Yes, Buddy. Try and get some sleep. Mom and Dad won't leave your side, you can rest now," I tell him, wishing I could take his place. I kiss him and lie down on the chair. As I close my eyes, I imagine his skull being opened and his brain exposed. I reach over and stroke his bald head, avoiding the scars that are already there, wondering where the new one will be.

In the deep of pain, I imagine that the tumor will be removed and we will go back to life. I imagine Gavin playing T-ball again, and playing tag. I imagine being with Grace and Gage, and not leaving them abruptly to save their brother. Within a few minutes, I am blessed with sleep. My only break from reality.

In the morning, Dr. Petronio walks in with the consent form, and discusses his plan and approach for surgery. He decides to go in from the base of Gavin's head. He wants to remove tumor tissue away from the brain stem. He tells us he will get as much as possible. We naively hope he will get all of it, knowing that's unlikely. He explains the risks which include infection, bleeding, blood clots, seizures, and brain swelling. We know without surgery, the bully will take over, so I try my best to look past them.

Like before, one of us can go into the operating room with Gavin as he falls asleep. I put the garb on and walk with Gavin's surgical team down the long hallway over to United Hospital, where the MRI suite is located. The surgical unit is large, with many people dressed and ready to open my son's head. I feel weak in my knees as I walk with them into the OR.

We try to distract him until the anesthesiologist nods to me that he is ready to push the sedation medicine in Gavin's IV. I hold Gavin's hand and nod back to him. As the white medicine is pushed through his veins, he tenses up and screams out, an unexpected response. With scared eyes, I look up at the team, who assure me he won't remember it. Tears fall down the side of his face as his body goes limp. I whisper in his ear.

"I love you baby, Mommy is here."

The last thing I will remember, is him crying out, eyes rolling back into his head. I am physically sick as nurse Shannon tells me I can kiss him one more time. I lean over and kiss his soft cheek, not wanting to leave. I am assured they will take good care of him and update often. Nurse Connie takes my cell number, and I am escorted out of the OR.

Nicole Pierson

In the waiting area, there are about twenty of us. My aunt Theresa brought bagels and coffee. She is the oldest sister, and takes on that role well. She is the caretaker, the peacekeeper, and since I was a child, she has always made me feel like one of her own. Jim and Jody, Steve's parents, sit with us and make small talk. They will be taking Grace and Gage while Gavin recovers. Jody asks me, "So how did it go?"

As I tell her about how Gavin screamed out, and went limp, her eyes fill with tears. She hates to hear about the suffering Gavin has to endure. It breaks her. And just as I feel helpless watching it firsthand, she too wishes none of this was happening.

I pace around everyone or read on my phone. I talk a little, but mostly sit quietly, breathing in and out. The first phone call comes about two hours after I left Gavin. They have made an incision and are beginning surgery. During the first two hours, I am told they have placed a central and arterial line and performed a pre-op MRI. I imagine Gavin's skull being drilled into. I don't want to imagine it but I can't stop.

I know I need to be alone, so I find a restroom and lock it behind me. I realize that on the other side of this wall is the OR. Gavin is right there, close enough I can almost feel him. I put my hands onto the wall, close my eyes, and sob so hard that I am shaking. I pray God is with Gavin. As scared as I am, I suddenly feel calm wash over me. It's strong enough to stop my tears and allow me to make my way back to my family.

I find a spot next to my sister Laura, and hold my phone. They said they will call every hour with an update. It's been twenty-three minutes. I find a tiny bit of comfort that to

Gavin, it will seem like seconds. But out here, those seconds feel like hours.

The updates come regularly, every hour just as I was promised. This saves me. About ten minutes before each hour has passed, I pace and stare at my phone, willing it to ring. I make sure my ringer is all the way up, just to be sure I don't miss a call.

My family understood what was going on in my mind and knew to just let me be. When the calls came in, the room, which was usually loud with all of us talking, would instantly silence as they tried to read my body language and tone. There was usually a sigh of relief, but sometimes just more silence, hoping the next call would be better.

"Shhh, it's ringing," I tell them as I hold my phone.

"Hello?" I answer quickly.

"Hi, this is Shannon. Gavin is doing well and is stable. Dr. Petronio is still working on the tumor. It will be awhile," she explains.

"Thank you," I reply before hanging up.

Eleven hours later, I was told that Dr. Petronio was closing. As each hour passed, I couldn't believe how long it was taking. The updates saved me though, knowing he was stable. I didn't know how much tumor Dr. Petronio was able to get, but I knew he got what he could. We moved to the intensive care unit waiting area, where we would meet him. The night sky was dark, and the silence deafening.

OUTSIDE OF THE Pediatric Intensive Care Unit (PICU), the beeping of the machines is louder and louder until it stops by the doors. I look over and see a bandage, tubes, machines, and nurses. Gavin is in there too. They pause for a moment before walking him inside. I have to wait.

Dr. Petronio finds us and tells us the surgery went well. "There were no complications and Gavin was stable the entire time," he explained. He was able to get what he could from the angle he performed the surgery. Gavin will have a quick MRI in the morning to check the tumor and swelling. We thanked him for the many hours, and headed to Gavin's room.

Steve and I held hands as we opened the curtain. Gavin is lifeless, with a ventilator still down his throat breathing for him. His eyes and cheeks look puffy and a white bandage wraps around his head. I have never seen so many machines. Hoppy helps soften the blow I feel seeing him like this. I make my way over to kiss him on his puffy cheek, walking through and around nurses.

The intensivist tells us he will keep Gavin sedated overnight until after the MRI. It is now after 2:00 a.m. Knowing Gavin will not be waking up until at least tomorrow, I hold his hand a few minutes before deciding to get some sleep. Despite so much of Gavin being covered in wires, tubes, and bandages, his hand looks the same. I hold it to my cheek, hoping he knows I am right here. And that I never left.

The next few hours are critical. All of the risks that could happen, could still happen. While Gavin's brain absorbs the shock of surgery, complications could arise. I cannot even go there. I go to sleep, telling myself that everything will be okay.

"Please God, can everything just be okay?"

Chapter Eight

And the peace of God,
    which transcends all understanding,
will guard your hearts
    and your minds in Christ Jesus.

Philippians 7

THE MORNING SUN tells me it is time. Gavin is being brought to radiology for a quick MRI. It is called quick, because it consists of just a few pictures that look for major problems such as swelling or bleeding. After the MRI, the intensivist tells us everything looks good. I am ecstatic to hear these words. "I am going to shut the sedation off and he should slowly wake up," he explains.

He stops the drip of medicine keeping Gavin awake. Gavin's eyes open first. Slowly, he looks around, quickly realizing he does not want this tube down his throat for one more second. He points to the tube frantically.

"Okay Gavin, we are going to take the tube out now," the doctor tells him. The tube is slowly pulled out, and Gavin coughs, as they encourage him to.

"I want Root Beer," he says in a raspy voice. Thank God he's back. Gavin wins for now, Joe Bully.

We slowly introduce water, and just enjoy hearing Gavin's voice again. He seems to be completely aware of the fact that he had brain surgery, and seems to have dodged all of the horrible things that could have happened. The plan is to slowly get Gavin moving again, with the help of physical and occupational therapy.

By the end of the day, Gavin sat up in his bed, and stood for a few minutes. His neck is very sore. The surgeon went through many muscles in his neck to get to the base of his brain. He is taking valium for the muscle soreness. His incision is itchy and we are careful when we help him sit up, or reposition in bed. I am hopeful that enough of the bully was removed to stop the pressure that was causing the breathing problems and other symptoms recently.

Although this is a victory, we feel lost as to what our new plan actually is. We threw away our original roadmap when the tumor grew. We went straight to brain surgery because there were no other options. Knowing Gavin needed the surgery to save his life was the only thing on our minds. As he recovers, we begin to shift our focus to our next move.

IT HAS BEEN nearly a week since Dr. Petronio had to cut through Gavin's brain to get to the bully. He was able to remove about 30% of the tumor and sent tissue samples to pathology. Gavin has been getting stronger every day, working hard with the therapists. This morning, the bandage was removed and I peeked at the new scar. It begins at the back of his head and goes down to the middle of his neck, about 4 inches long.

Gavin's breathing has been better since the ER trip. The surgery likely has helped with his breathing, as his brain stem now has room to function properly. We are told the tumor was pressing against this, making it flat like a pancake rather than a fist like it should be. The brainstem is responsible for things like breathing, heart rate, and sleeping. These are basic, imperative things needed to survive.

The thoughts build quickly in my mind, making it hard to breathe. I can feel the fear in everything I do. It is there when a machine beeps differently, or Gavin has a headache. There are so many things that have, and still can, go wrong because the tumor is still growing in Gavin's brain. The fear is easy to feel and embrace, however it is hope that gets us through the day. This morning I went for a walk to United Hospital, which is connected to Children's. In the gift shop, I found a picture that said, "We must choose HOPE over fear." It was the perfect gift for my soul, reminding me I cannot let the fear take over. If I do, we will lose for sure.

Devastation and motivation go hand in hand these days. I have to do something more. I keep thinking this, over and over again. This tumor will not give in easily. It is powerful, and wants to win. Adrenaline kicks me into high gear. I use the little bit of hope I have, and consciously put it first. We did not remove the entire tumor. It will continue to grow. I know we need more, I just have to find it.

GAVIN SPENDS MOST of his time in bed watching movies. He remembers every line, even if he has only heard it once or twice. Every day he requests music therapy and dog visits. Yesterday, he even got a massage. He kicked me out, saying he wants it quiet with some calm music. I found some piano music and downloaded it onto his iPad. Child Life brings crafts for him, but he never does them. His fine motor skills and lack of interest puts crafts at the bottom of the list. I take them anyways, just in case.

Physical Therapy and Occupational Therapy continue to come in daily. Cindy, a petite and motivated physical therapist, has been working with him the past few days. She has the ability to make him work hard, while he thinks he is just playing a game. He loves going for hunts with her around the PICU. The nurses love watching him walk around too. He always puts a smile on their faces.

Steve and I have mastered the art of avoiding lines and getting around with the IV pole. When Gavin walks around or does therapy, we have to clamp his drain that was put in after surgery to drain excess fluid. This is to avoid too much draining and a horrible headache. He doesn't complain about the bandage, the drain, and the hours he must lay in the same position.

"Mom, can we clamp my drain?" Gavin asks politely as I am reading a book. Nighttime meds are finished, which means the nurses will try to let Gavin rest. They have to check blood pressure and vitals every two hours and also watch his continuous monitor from right outside the room. But after the last meds of the day, it's quiet.

"Okay Buddy," I reply as I make my way over to him. His neck is getting sore and he needs help adjusting himself before he falls asleep. Despite the walks and therapy, his movement is limited. His gymnast muscles are fading as the steroids take over. In the past three days, he has gained four pounds. Where his collarbone usually protrudes, a layer of cushion has formed. We try to distract him so that he does not think about food. Dexamethasone, a steroid, is being given four times a day in high doses to keep brain swelling down. Every ten minutes, Gavin thinks he is starving. I tell myself this is only temporary. As I watch him struggle to get out of bed, I remember he was climbing trees just months ago.

As GAVIN IS falling asleep (not an easy task with all of the medications affecting him), a toddler nearby is crying. Gavin looks over to Steve and me with concern.

"Do you hear that?" he asks.

"Yeah, do you want me to put your music on so you can fall asleep?" Steve replies.

"No, it's not that. I just feel so bad for her," Gavin replies sweetly. His eyes fill with tears as he listens to the cries that have now become screams.

I look at the bandage around his head and the machines surrounding him. He cannot move unless his brain drain is clamped. If he does, he will instantly get a headache or vomit. He is fighting to live, with many moving parts to his recovery. Yet, he is worried about the crying child next door. At six years old, he shows more compassion than most. He cares so deeply for anyone suffering, wanting to do something to help and wishing he could make it better. My sweet boy who would do so much good in this world, is trying to stay alive. It's not fair. Finally, the screams stop and Gavin is able to fall asleep.

A thunderstorm shakes the windows as we try to sleep. The rain comes down violently against the roof, and the thunder interrupts my thoughts and worries. This startling response, ironically calms my soul. The storm going on inside of me is not as big as the one outside of the PICU window, which brings unexpected peace. It washes over me, and I realize God is bigger than my worries. He is bigger than Joe Bully. Although I cannot understand this life right now, I know God can. Be still, I tell myself as the thunder rolls.

We have been discussing what is next in Gavin's treatment. Oncology has mentioned trying a different chemotherapy. I feel in my heart this is not the right move. Not while that tumor still sits in Gavin's brain. The results of the biopsy show the tumor is only mature teratoma, which is benign, and chemotherapy does not often stop a benign tumor from growing.

Benign sounds like a friendly word, but in Gavin's case it isn't. If it was cancerous, we could shrink it and then remove all of it. Because it is benign, surgical removal is the only cure. The problem is the tumor is buried deep in Gavin's brain and it is huge. We schedule a second craniotomy, hoping Dr. Petronio can remove more tumor safely. Before Gavin can fully recover from the first surgery, he will undergo another.

Knowing our only option is dangerous surgery, I continue to research. I tell myself that we need another surgery to give Gavin's brain more space, and after that, we will find something. There has to be a cure out there.

WITH THE FOURTH of July in three days, we are hoping to get out of here and be home a little bit before the surgery, but Joe Bully has other plans. Routine blood tests are showing Gavin's BUN and white blood cell counts are high. This could mean infection and a host of other things. Today Gavin will have a chest X-ray, abdominal X-ray, blood cultures, urinalysis, and an EKG. His heart rate and blood pressure are high too. After telling him we may go home, I have to tell him we aren't.

"Gavin, your body just isn't better yet," I tell him, knowing he will understand what it means.

"So, we aren't going home." he states with his head down.

"No, Buddy. We have to stay," I whisper dismally.

He is quiet, and I can see he is crushed at the moment. He was so excited to see his cousins Sam and Logan. He wanted to go to Pancake Island on Uncle Reed's boat, and eat the delicious food and treats he knows Aunt Theresa always has.

He wanted to be a kid.

Watching him melt into himself and seeing the sadness in his heart, I try to conjure up something that will help. I tell him we will have popsicles and go outside tomorrow, and on the Fourth of July, maybe we can watch the fireworks from the rooftop. I actually have not yet asked if all of this is even possible, but I will beg the nurses and doctors later. He tries to smile, letting me know he understands.

After pressure was lifted off his brainstem, everything has been a little off. His oxygen is better, but other things worse. We have added more medications. The steroids are in control. Ham and cheese sandwiches, and Snickers are everywhere to prove it. I try to distract him, but eating is his only pleasure. The side effects of some medications may be causing some of these new issues, which is frustrating.

We are trying to help Gavin's brain regulate his body effectively. On the bright side, his G-tube is coming in handy with all of the new medications. If they are disgusting, like

Nicole Pierson

potassium and sodium phosphate, we can just put them directly into his stomach. He thinks it's pretty cool that he doesn't even have to taste them yet they still go into his stomach. He has the ability to look at things for what they are, rather than what they represent, which is something I need to learn to do. When I look at the G-tube coming out of Gavin's stomach, I wonder if he will need it forever and how we will ever beat this brain tumor. He just sees it as a way to get out of gross medicine.

After we both accepted we were here to stay, we focus on whatever positive we can. Our family and friends have been coordinating a golf benefit happening today. We had hoped Gavin would be in attendance. The date was set when we thought we had a plan, before we realized the tumor was growing uncontrollably. Steve, Grace, and Gage, are there, and I stay with Gavin.

They FaceTime us a few times throughout the event. During dinner, Steve brings his phone around so Gavin can wave at everyone. I am in awe of the people supporting us. I can see their expressions change when they see the condition Gavin is in. Many people have not seen him in the past few weeks. He has chubby cheeks, an eye patch, a bandage on his head, scars, and tubes. I am sure it's hard to look at. I have seen all of this in slow motion, taking one blow at a time. They look at him in somewhat disbelief, coupled with heartache. I pretend I do not see their expression, while Gavin smiles and waves.

When we end our FaceTime session, Gavin looks at me with a smile. "Wow Mom! So many people care about me!"

"Yes they do, and they want you to beat Joe Bully," I reply.

I CUDDLE UP in Gavin's bed as he drifts off for an afternoon nap. I hold him tight, carefully leaning my head near his. I wish that I knew I could hold him forever. I lie there still and my eyes become heavy.

As I arrive, I feel as if everyone is looking at me. I am not sure why. The leaves on the ground are wet, and the sky is grey. My footsteps are sluggish as I make my way to the door of the funeral home. I cannot see anyone's face, but I know them. They are blurry for some reason.

As I am about to open the door, it opens for me. An older man holds the door and says, "Right this way Mrs. Pierson." I think to myself, how nice is he to address me by name. I hang up my coat, and follow the man to be seated, I think.

Instead, he takes me to some kind of private room.

As I approach a casket, I notice it is small. I suddenly panic and ask the man where my children are. I feel sick. He looks at me sorrowfully, and says, "Remember Mrs. Pierson, Grace and Gage are with Steve, we already went through this." I look at him and try to remember what he is talking about. I have no recollection.

"Do you need more time?" he asks politely. Now I am beginning to get angry. Surely he must be confused, and he forgot to tell me Gavin was with Steve too. Why am I even in here? I start to feel claustrophobic and my palms are clammy. He waits for answer, but suddenly I realize I know.

I remember. Oh God, no. I walk quickly to the casket, praying it cannot be. As I peek inside, blonde hair appears. Gavin is dressed in a black suit, with a blue vest matching his blue bunny next to him. I start to remember what happened.

He stopped breathing.

Nicole Pierson

They couldn't save him. I held him for hours until they pried his lifeless body from mine. Part of my soul left with him. The bully has won.

I fall to my knees and grab for his hand. He cannot squeeze back. I shout, "Gavin, oh sweet boy, I am so sorry. I am so sorry that I couldn't save you!" I sob until I have produced all the tears my body can. I don't want to leave him. I cannot put his body in the ground. I just want to hold him a little longer.

Someone is behind me, gently tapping my shoulder, telling me it's time. I want to lie down with him and never wake up. The pain is too immense. They tap again, this time a little harder to get my attention. "I'm not ready to let go!" I shout.

My eyes pop open and my cheeks are wet. I am in the hospital bed, Gavin's warm body next to mine. He is okay. He is waking up too, and the nurse who is standing at my bedside asks if I am all right.

"Yes, I am fine, just a nightmare," I reply as I wipe my face, still trying to grasp what is real, my heart pounding out of my chest.

"I was just waking you to let you know they are ready to do Gavin's ultrasound in Radiology," she says softly.

Before we head down, I look at Gavin's sweet face, and his beautiful blue eyes. I kiss his forehead, then each cheek, and put my cheek to his. I close my eyes and repeat to myself, "He is alive." I take deep, steady breaths as we head down to Radiology. It scares me how real my nightmare felt. For the next few days, I hug and kiss Gavin incessantly and pray he never leaves me. I cannot bury my child. God, please don't make me bury my child.

A RED, WHITE, and blue lei hangs off Gavin's wheelchair as we push him through the skyway. I was able to convince the nurses and doctors that Gavin desperately needed some kind of Fourth of July. A flag he made today in the playroom is in his hand because I finally convinced him to do a craft. He is ready to celebrate and watch some fireworks. My friend Emmie, and her son Brad, came up to watch them with Steve and me.

"I have never seen them so close to the capital building," I tell Gavin as we approach the gold parking ramp. We are all trying to pretend this is normal, keeping conversation light and the focus on making Gavin smile.

As we get to the roof of the parking ramp, we put the brakes on Gavin's wheelchair. It was too long of a walk for him, and he has a drain coming out of his brain, so walking wasn't feasible. But hey, we did convince the floor doctor to let us come here in this condition, so we are not complaining.

The nurse gave us a couple of popsicles, and the boys are eating them quickly because it is very warm, even at almost ten at night. Gavin watches the fireworks burst in front of him as he drips sticky syrup on his pajamas. Some of it gets on his white bandage, and I begin to wipe it until I remember they will be giving him a new one tomorrow, so I stop.

When the grand finale is complete, Gavin looks at us and says, "This is the best Fourth of July ever!" Emmie, Steve, and I look at each other and no words are needed. Steve says, "I'm glad you liked them Gavin," as he unlocks the wheels and we make our way back. I am reminded how different life is through a child's eyes. He has never seen fireworks from a rooftop before or at the state capitol. It didn't matter that he was having another brain surgery in the morning. To him, this was life. He didn't have expectations that could be let down, or dreams that were broken. He was here, right now, enjoying

Nicole Pierson

this moment. What if everyone shared his perspective, I wonder. What if, rather than getting upset when things did not turn out as we had planned, we just enjoyed what did happen and were thankful?

Gavin is helping me realize I can still find joy, even if that joy is not what I imagined. His joy for each moment, regardless of the circumstances, is inspiring. He is teaching me to be thankful in any situation. As we get back to his room, the excitement drifts away, reminding us what we must face in the morning. Joe Petronio verses Joe Bully, round two.

"Thanks Mom and Dad for taking me to see the fireworks," Gavin says as we help him back into bed.

"You're welcome, Gav. I love you Bud," Steve replies.

I sit by Gavin's bed until he falls asleep. Residual fireworks still light up the distant sky as I head to the couch and close the blinds. I pretend the fireworks are shooting stars—I could use a wish right now.

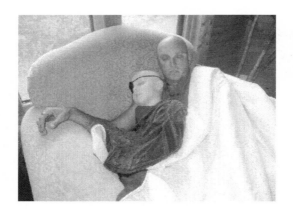

Steve and Gavin on Father's Day 2012

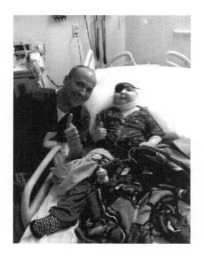

Gavin and Nurse Travis July 2012

Nicole Pierson

Chapter Nine

Be still and know that I am God.

Psalm 46:10

THE MORNING CAME quickly, anxiety its shadow. From the moment Gavin woke up he has been off. I wish I did not have to continue to put him through scans, pokes, and surgeries. The alternative is we lose him. We wheel him down to Radiology with hope this won't always be his reality, and one day, he will be cured.

The MRI proves to be difficult for Gavin. He is hungry, but cannot eat. During the scan, he was in tears because his knees felt achy. They hurt when he lays down, I believe due to the extra weight. Also, the bandage is itching his head, and he has to be completely still, which is difficult. The drain must be draining a little fast which is giving him a headache.

I am taking many deep breaths and try to be encouraging so we can just get it done. The MRI technicians do their best to make him comfortable and get through the scan, but it is horrible. I am beyond frustrated he has experienced so much anxiety right before surgery.

After an hour, we are done trying. I am not entirely sure the scans are good enough to use anyways because of all of the stopping and moving. We may have just put him through all of it for nothing. I thank the technicians for trying, and we head to the OR. Once in the unit, I am given consent forms by Dr. Petronio. Today, Gavin's incision will be at the top of his head. Dr. Petronio explains that when it grew, the tumor displaced major cerebral veins. They are not in their normal anatomical place, causing increased pressure on them as well.

He explains he will avoid them, but tells us that there is a chance of stroke. Worse, there is a chance Gavin will not make it through the surgery.

"I wish there was another way, but it seems there isn't," he says apologetically.

It is gut wrenching to sign my name. It feels as if I am both fighting and giving up at the same time. With each letter I write, different scenarios flood my mind. Will I regret signing this if he has a stroke and is bound to a wheelchair for the rest of his life? Would I regret it if we did nothing, and he died?

I would never forgive myself.

I continue to sign, my heart bleeding with each letter, knowing it's the only way he has a chance at living. I don't even know how we got to this point, standing here with my body shaking in the OR. I feel trapped, knowing this is our only choice. I never thought it would be so hard to sign a piece of paper. As I finish and hand the clipboard back to him, I suddenly want to take it back. I have developed a lump in my throat, so large I feel as if everyone can see it. I hope I am not asked one more question, because my knees will surely buckle and down I will go.

"I love you, Gavin," is all I can manage, as he is rolled into the operating room. Steve grabs his hand just as they disappear beyond my sight. A clicking sound has brought my attention to the double doors, leading me away from Gavin. The nurse is there, waiting to walk me out so they can open my child's skull again. I am supposed to go, knowing I may not see my child alive again. How can I walk forward? As eyes are on me, I calmly exit.

"We will keep you updated every hour, like last time," the nurse assures me. I nod, and walk aimlessly. I so badly want to run back and give Gavin just one more kiss. Tell him one more time that I love him to the moon and back. I turn back, but the doors are closed. The hall, so bright and inanimate, feels as if it has eyes too. I walk slowly to the waiting area and find my family. I sit and quietly look at my phone, wishing for a final update. "If I could, I would be sedated alongside Gavin," I joked with the anesthesiologist this morning, but he didn't laugh. I was totally serious.

Steve comes out and tells us Gavin's sedation was smooth. A tiny comfort. We know we will hear from the team in a couple of hours so we do whatever we can to pass the time. It takes a while to get set up and do a scan, so the first update takes longer.

"Hello," I answer quickly.

"Hi Nicole. Gavin is stable, but he did lose a lot of blood. He needed a blood transfusion and surgery has now started," the nurse explains. Everyone is listening, reading my tone and hanging on to every word I speak. When I hang up,

I stare down, taking a long breath before repeating what I had just heard.

"He is stable now but he lost a lot of blood. He needed a transfusion and they have just started surgery," I say with my head down, letting everyone know I can't say another word.

We all know how bad it is. We all know how much worse it could get. Powerless. It is how every person in this room feels at the moment. It's not like the time a few summers ago when we all sat on my deck and suddenly heard screaming. One of the kids let go of the wagon with a few others inside. They tumbled towards a family of sticker bushes.

All of the women jumped up and ran over to help. It took hours to get the stickers out of Grace and Molly's hair. The women in my family panic first and calm down later. We are ready to intervene and save the day, sometimes when we don't really need to. My sister Missy and I, along with our cousins Jen and Steph, used to poke fun at our moms when we were kids. They always jumped, quite literally, to the worst case scenarios. We forgave them, as we realized why they were that way. Their sister, my Aunt Laura, whom I never met, was hit by a car and killed at just twelve years old. Up until then, they believed they were all invincible. At such a young age, they learned their oldest sister was not.

Now that we are all mothers, we are the same. We hear a cry and all of us jump up to help. Overprotective maybe, but it pained us to see our children hurting. We are mama bears and would do anything for our children. Yet, we all sit here today and cannot help Gavin. He might die. We are not easily silenced, but you could hear a pin drop.

Nicole Pierson

As soon as I hang up the phone, I set my timer for an hour. As we sit in United Hospital's surgery waiting area, I watch the screen of patient names, surgery start and end times, and status. Gavin's name is again the only one on the screen. Other families come and go, as we continue to wait. Our last update was that an intraoperative scan showed no stroke, and it would be several more hours. I am relieved there was no stroke. I push away my vivid nightmare from a few days ago and keep praying.

This bully is not going down easily. They are still working on him, and it is now 11:00 p.m. I cannot believe he has been under sedation so long. I have not heard his sweet voice for fifteen hours. My hope that all of the tumor could be removed today, is dwindling. I will be happy if my child comes out of surgery without complications. Breathing, so that I can hug him again. As I stare at my phone, all of the possible updates cycle through my head. I keep praying everything is okay, and minute by minute, the hour is almost over. They should be calling. Why aren't they calling?

"Hello," I answer quickly and apprehensively.

"Dr. Petronio is closing. You can go to the PICU waiting area, and he will come talk to you when he is done," the nurse explains.

DR. PETRONIO'S TIRED footsteps alert us to greet him. We sit down with him in the waiting area as Gavin is wheeled by, unconscious. Just seeing him, even for a few seconds, calms me.

Dr. Petronio tries to take us through the day, all twenty-two hours of it. He believes he has removed the tumor tissue that was pressing against the cerebral veins. "I thought

I had gotten what I could from the angle I approached and was ready to close. But, a new plane appeared, and it was like I was being guided to more of the tumor," he explains. When this new line of sight opened, he continued for hours.

I get the feeling that this sort of thing doesn't happen often in neurosurgery. The way that he explained it, I would guess this has never happened before. In brain surgery, everything is mapped out, and the MRI gives the information needed to carry out the plan. This new plane, not anticipated, allowed him to continue. All day I had prayed, "God, please let your hands work through Dr. Petronio's hands." Chills spread through my body as I listen.

He hopes Gavin does okay and says we will see how he is in the morning. Until then, he will remain sedated and on a ventilator, like last time. Neurosurgeons do their best work, and know the brain well, but Joe Bully was pushing Gavin's brain out of the way. Our hope is he wakes up and recovers well.

"Thank you for everything," Steve says as he shakes his hand.

"You're welcome, I will be by tomorrow to check on him," he assures.

"Good night, I hope you're able to get some well-deserved rest," I add as he walks away.

We wait for a nurse to come get us and bring us to Gavin. After what seems like forever, the doors open. Walking in, I offer an exhausted nod to the nurses at the front desk. They return my gesture with half-smiles, sad to see Gavin again. We focus on getting to his room, bracing ourselves for what we will see again.

I ignore things I don't want to give attention to. I hold Gavin's hand and for a moment, I am at peace knowing the worst did not happen. My moment of relief doesn't last long as the nurse shows me his tummy. He was in a prone position, which means laying on his stomach, during surgery. He developed a large blister on his abdomen, something the surgical team does their best to avoid. The many hours of laying in the same position has caused this. It is hard to look at, and I assume it will be very painful when Gavin wakes up. It looks like the shape of a kidney and is probably about the same size if not bigger. The nurse explains that she will watch it carefully and tells us to get some rest.

IT IS LATE morning, and Gavin is having a post-op scan to check for swelling or bleeding before they take out the breathing tube and wake him up from sedation. He has now been sedated for over twenty-four hours. I yearn to hear his sweet voice.

The scan shows normal post-op swelling, but nothing of concern. The intensivist begins the wake-up process. He lowers the sedation medication, and Gavin slowly starts to move. After brain surgery, the patient must be monitored closely for neurological changes. We watch intently, and see him move his left leg. Then his left arm. Then the other side of his body moves slowly. Finally, he was awake enough to open his eyes and point to the tube, all of this happening over a span of about ten minutes. Once he gets to this point he is aware he wants it out. Now!

The doctor tells Gavin he will be taking the tube out, and I cringe as he counts to three. I close my eyes and pray it goes quickly. Soon Gavin is coughing, and I am at his side.

There are some things I can watch, but this is not one of them. I grab some swabs and a small cup of water so that I can moisten his mouth. His mouth is so dry and he moans in appreciation as I gently swab it.

"Did… we.. get all of… Joe… Bully?" he asks in a hoarse, squeaky voice. Thank God he can talk.

It pains me to tell him we didn't. Not even close. I tell him we got a lot of Joe Bully, but he is still there. I tell him that we will keep fighting Joe Bully until he is gone. He does not say much when I respond to his question. He just nods, and I think he's still waking up, or maybe just doesn't like my answer. I can't imagine how he feels right now after more than twenty-four hours of sedation.

Throughout the day, I keep thinking he will wake up like he did last time. He says a couple things but then seems distant. I mention my concern to the doctor, who tells me he may just be taking longer to feel awake. My intuition tells me otherwise. I feel like something is wrong.

The next morning, the neurosurgery team comes by to check on him. They are pleased he is awake, eating, and that his vitals have been good. I mention that Gavin hasn't been himself, barely starting a conversation and not responding when we talk to him. They assure me this can be normal and should improve in a couple of days.

BY DAY FOUR, I know it's more than that, and convince the nurse that it has not improved. She seems to understand more than anyone I had talked to yet, and decides to try something.

"Gavin, what is your favorite color?" she asks from a distance, out of his view. She makes sure not to look at him as to cue him. Gavin continues to watch TV, and does not give any type of response. It's like she wasn't talking at all.

Then she walks carefully around his IV pole, to behind his bed, and begins to snap her fingers.

"Who is snapping?" Gavin says, slightly annoyed.

She stops and walks back around to him with a smile.

"Gavin, what is your favorite color?" she asks, with again no response.

Together, we pinpoint exactly what is going on. He could hear sounds. Snapping, airplanes outside, and the beeping of the machines. Yet, when we talked to him, it was like we were speaking a different language. All he was hearing was noise.

The first day post-op, he would at least attempt to engage in conversation. Now he sits quietly most of the time, not wanting to try. Imagine waking up to a world you suddenly cannot understand. Lord, has he not been through enough? Now he has to continue this journey and not even know what is going on? The thought is crippling.

I tell him I love him.

He stares off as if I've said nothing at all.

Chapter Ten

Faith.
It does not make things easy
it makes them possible.

Luke 1:37

AFTER HOURS OF brain surgery, all I wanted to do was tell him how much I loved him, and how brave he was. But he was lost. He is probably wondering why we all changed while he was in surgery. He is trying to understand a world that makes little sense. It must be like waking up in a different country where everyone is speaking a language you cannot comprehend.

It must be why he has stopped trying.

As he watches *The Lorax* again, the nurses buzz around him. He has seen the movie a few times and is smiling for the first time since waking up. His eyes are focused, eyebrows scrunched in anticipation.

"You wouldn't hit a woman!" Gavin says exactly at the right time. He laughs hysterically afterwards as the characters continue on with their lines. A few other times throughout the movie, he says the lines from memory. When he is able to chime in at the right parts, his face lights up. He feels a part of this world again.

For a moment he hears, even if it is because his brain remembers the part of the movie. It's fascinating his brain can recall movie lines, yet not understand words. I wish I could say something to him and he would hear it, but for now, this is enough to get us through the day. He knows I'm here, holding his hand. He turns to me and our eyes meet. I smile, and I know he knows. Thankfully he can read at a kindergarten level, so I write some words down. He can sort of read my lips and discern what I am saying by the tone of my voice. He guesses what I am asking until I shake my head yes. It works for now. After the movie is over, I stand in Gavin's view and tap his shoulder so that he knows I am going to talk to him. I move my lips slowly.

"Do I want to go outside?" he asks. I shake my head no.

"Do I want to play?" he tries again. I put my fingers together as to say he's close to figuring it out. I then decide to try charades. I pretend to run, and then I walk with my arms swinging. I am sure I look crazy to anyone passing by.

"Oh, do I want to go for a walk?" he says excitedly.

"Yes!" I say as I shake my head with a smile.

I am hopeful I will soon know more about why he cannot understand us, and what we can do about it. After our walk, the nurse tells me a speech therapist is on her way to evaluate Gavin. I prepare all of my research I have gathered over the past few days while everyone thought he was fine, and stand up to greet her when she walks in.

Be Strong and Brave

Tricia, a bubbly and straightforward therapist, walks into the room for his evaluation. I can tell she is going to help figure out what is going on. First, we discuss his behavior. She listens closely while also taking notes as I describe the past few days. I tell her about the snapping incident, and share what I've read. From what I could gather, I thought it might be Wernicke's aphasia.

She explains Wernicke's aphasia, and points out his expressive speech is perfectly normal. With Wernicke's aphasia, he would not always make sense when he speaks. Also, if he can read words, which he shows her he can, this diagnosis doesn't quite fit. She begins her evaluation. Without giving him any visual cues she asks some questions.

"Gavin, how many sisters do you have?" No response. He turns and looks at her blankly, wishing he could understand. Then I try.

"Gavin," I wait until he is looking at me. I slowly say "Grace," then point to him. Finally, I say "sister." He replies "Yes, Grace is my sister." I then find some pictures on my phone from our recent Wisconsin Dells trip, point to each one, waiting for him to say something.

"That's my cousins, Bradley and Lyndsey," he says, looking at the picture of them coming out of the water slide. "And there is my little brother Gage and my sister Grace," he points. Tricia asks him, "How many days were you at Wisconsin Dells?" Now that he knows what topic we are on, he reads her lips and responds appropriately.

"We were there for four days," he says with confidence. Tricia notes that once he understands the subject, he compensates by lip-reading and possibly tone of voice to understand if it is a question or statement. She comments that he seems to understand me well, likely because he is familiar with how I talk.

After he demonstrates he can read words he previously learned without trouble, she decides to see how he does with music. We sing "If you're happy and you know it clap your hands," and as soon as it is time, Gavin claps his hands. He smiles, because he understands again. I am baffled he can hear, yet not hear at the same time. The brain is much more compartmentalized than I once thought. After the speech evaluation, Gavin is further referred to a neuropsychologist, Dr. Elizabeth Adams. He will see her outpatient, hopefully next week. Until then, we will do charades, use pictures, and write words he can read. Gavin can then guess what we are saying until he gets it right.

Despite not being able to communicate effectively, he is eager to go home. He was on twelve medications before the two brain surgeries, and in the past few weeks since he has been inpatient, seven more have been added. Today, Gavin had his brain drain removed, which helped get rid of extra fluid. He can finally move without having to get permission. One less thing attached—makes him a happy boy. While he walks a therapy dog with the physical therapist, I discuss plans for home with the doctor.

"Well, neuro says he is okay to go home tomorrow, however I would like his blood pressure to stay down and sodium levels to stay up," the doctor explains. We make a plan to adjust some meds and see how he does. I settle in, making the best of it. We do a nightly game of charades, one of the few games he can play, hoping to go home tomorrow.

TOMORROW COMES AND goes. Home keeps getting pushed to another "tomorrow." We have moved from PICU to the floor, but things are just not where they need to be yet. Today, I am able to convince them to give us a pass out of here. Our family and friends are having a benefit for Gavin and we decide to surprise them. As we walk in, I can see my Aunt Theresa's eyes fill with tears. Gavin smiles a lot. He sees friends from school, like his friend Brynn, and his cousins. He cannot understand what anyone is saying but is enjoying the time out of the hospital.

After a few hours, we have to go back to St. Paul. Luckily we were moved to the floor, and are out of PICU. We missed a visit from my school friend Raema, who left us a message of hope. I am sad I've missed her, as it's been years. Her words help me think about what is next on this journey. Two brain surgeries are behind us, but future plans are still being discussed.

Once we settle back in and Gavin falls asleep, I sit in silent reflection. The room is dark, and the halls are quiet. The nurses don't come in as often when we are not in PICU. Unfortunately, Joe Bully still resides in Gavin's brain, a constant companion we can't escape. He has planted himself quite comfortably next to Gavin's critical brain structures. I am beginning to think this tumor will never go away. Surgery is barely keeping up with the growth. Steroids are slowing it, but we need more than that. How will Gavin keep going through such long, dangerous brain surgeries?

Oncology has explained to me that if there are any immature cells (cancerous cells), we need to continue to address them with chemotherapy. Although the tumor markers are normal, microscopic cells may be present. When

Nicole Pierson

Oncology came in last week to give me this recommendation, I was tending to a child who cannot communicate, and was in a moment of agreement. However, I keep going back to the family resource center, and reading about Growing Teratoma Syndrome. I talk to my aunt Lisa, who explains all of the metabolic processes of this monster. The message is clear. Do not do chemo. In some cases, giving chemo resulted in faster growth. Although we do not want cancer cells to grow, Joe Bully is the immediate threat to his life.

If the tumor markers are normal, and the biopsies have all showed mature teratoma, we do not have proof any cancerous cells exist. The tumor doubled in size when Gavin had chemo. I just do not understand why we would give it more fuel. I ask the doctor on the floor to schedule a conference meeting with the team, including both Neurosurgery and Oncology, because my head is spinning and I need to clarify the plan going forward. I gather all of my research, and prepare to ask hard questions. The ones I have been avoiding for the past month. Dreading tomorrow, I try to fall asleep.

STEVE MEETS ME to attend the meeting. Gavin is with a volunteer, feeding the fish, as we head to a small conference room to meet the team. Not wanting to, but needing to, I begin the questions I fear to have answered.

"I am wondering how many surgeries you think Gavin will need?" I begin. I feel as if we have only talked about what's next, but not truly about a long term plan. The plan that cures Gavin.

We hear words like "quality of life," and "brain damage," and I am thinking this meeting was not the best idea.

Be Strong and Brave

I want to scream, but not at them. I feel as if they are piling rocks on me with every answer, and I am too weak to push them off and get up again. I feel paralyzed but somehow nod and continue to listen.

"If Gavin continues to have brain surgeries, he may have more time, but the surgery alone could add neurological damage," Dr. Petronio explains.

"I don't think you realize how bad it could have been," he continues, referring to the dangerous craniotomies he has already performed. I assured him that I do know how bad it could have been. I know Gavin could have died, or had a stroke. But he didn't, and I believe the reason for that is beyond what medical knowledge can tell any of us sitting in this room.

"My hope is that a third surgery could give him years," he finishes.

This cannot be happening. I thought our goal was a cure, not just giving him a couple of years! Are we not on the same page? Don't they understand I want my son to have more than a few years? Why are they talking like this? I had never given up hope he will survive. I am reminded, there is no cure and there may come a time when there is nothing more that can be done. The people who can save him are telling me we can only hope for years.

My soul is shattered and part of me died with this news. I want more than years. He is only six years old damn it! I want him to grow up, is that too much to ask?

We leave the meeting with a tentative third craniotomy date, and broken hearts. Reluctantly, I understand their words, as much as they hurt. Research backs up what they are saying. The tumor is difficult to remove and will continue to grow. Without removing the entire thing, Gavin will eventually die. Unless we find a miracle, a cure—we will lose this fight.

I think about the children who have lost their battles and realize I never imagined Gavin being one of them. Even after his diagnosis, and even after it became a giant, I still thought he would be the one to beat the odds. As we walk back to Gavin's room, I am destroyed. I do not understand how my feet keep moving or how my breaths continue to give me life. Without knowing what I will say, I turn to Steve outside of Gavin's room. A little boy hooked up to an IV pole is walking by, so I wait for him to pass.

"It's not fair!" I say in tears. Steve hugs me and listens. He knows I need to cry, and be angry, and break down.

"I can't watch him die!" I continue, trying to stop crying and trying to be quiet so Gavin would not hear me.

"I know. I can't either," he says before Gavin calls out from his bed, spotting us. I wipe tears and breathe a few quick breaths before walking in.

"I got to feed the fish!" he exclaims excitedly. While he was busy sprinkling food on the surface of the water, giving life to the fish, we were listening to the doctors, hearing that there is no cure for his life. Until we are discharged, I think about how to change the words coming from the doctor's mouths—how to change Gavin's fate.

AT HOME, GAVIN has been walking more each day. He still cannot understand what anyone is saying. We have all gotten very good at charades and Pictionary. Tonight we went to see the new *Ice Age* movie at the theatre. Gavin laughed and ate popcorn. I have never enjoyed a movie as much as I did tonight. I don't think I even really watched the movie. I watched my three children, and for a little while, I forgot.

I forgot that my child has no cure, and that at best, he has years.

Tomorrow we will meet with Neurosurgery, Oncology, and the Neuropsychologist. In the past few days, I have compiled research articles and clinical trials I plan to bring up. Knowing the medical team does not have a cure, I am desperate to find one. I talk to my aunt Lisa, who is helping me look for something that might work. Being a pediatric doctor, she has access to resources I don't. She has called a few people to get more information for me, and when I feel like I am drowning, she brings me to the surface again.

I am impressed with Gavin's efforts. He has begun to find creative ways to figure out what everyone around him is saying. After the movie, I look to the back seat and see him counting with his fingers, while talking to Grace. I mouthed "What are you doing with your fingers?" while pointing to my own fingers, to cue him.

"I am counting the syllables," he tells me.

"Steve, did you hear that?" I say with astonishment.

"Yeah, I did. Wow, he's determined isn't he?" he replies.

He is counting the syllables of Grace's words. She says them slower so he can do this. What a smart and compassionate little girl she is. Patiently, she says one word at a time while he counts. He came up with this strategy on his own and I am in awe watching him execute it. I remember when Mrs. Protivinsky, his kindergarten teacher, discussed learning about syllables at his last conference. Thankfully, he finally picked it up. I am sure she would be proud to know how he's using it. He does not give up easily and loves to chat. I believe his drive and motivation will help him communicate in some meaningful way.

DR. ADAMS, THE neuropsychologist, is a petite, well-spoken woman, who is passionate about her work. She begins by explaining what she will be looking for and is very informative. She has Gavin read a few sentences and identify objects from pictures. She then plays different noises, like a duck and a train for Gavin to name. She is impressed with how well he does those tasks. Finally, we begin the task we know he will struggle with. She asks him questions without visual cues and he stares at her. He says, "I don't understand if you are asking a question." She takes notes as she continues with different tests.

Next, a functional MRI scan is done. Gavin looks at pictures while his brain activity is recorded. The area of the brain that is supposed to light up does. Lastly, he listens to words without a picture, and the part of the brain that processes language remains inactive. Her diagnosis is that he has pure word deafness, also called auditory agnosia. She explains to me that the tumor was pressing on Gavin's left temporal lobe before surgery, which is used to process sounds into meaning. She believes this pressure was likely causing some disruption, however, Gavin was using a backup, via the corpus callosum, to process language. She has a way of making me feel like I understand the intricacies of the brain.

During surgery, the only way to get to the tumor was by cutting the many fibers of the corpus callosum. This consists of millions of fibers connecting the left and right hemispheres—it is the communication pathway between them. Dr. Adams hypothesizes when the tumor pressed on the temporal lobe, Gavin likely relied on the corpus callosum to process information, specifically, spoken language. Now, he doesn't have that route.

The tumor still presses on the temporal lobe, meaning there is a small possibility once that is lifted, he could recover. The literature is scarce. Pure word deafness occurs in older stroke patients, and only a few children are documented with the disorder. Full recovery is unheard of, at least in the literature and to Dr. Adams knowledge. The way in which Gavin developed it gives us some hope though. There are so many unknowns and possibilities, but one thing is clear. He needs to have a way to communicate. Dr. Adams recommends he learn sign language, which means our entire family is going to learn sign language.

I am devastated after hearing a diagnosis. I wanted it, but I had hoped there would be treatment. Holding back tears as she thoroughly explains all of this, I manage to ask her, "Will he ever be able to comprehend language again?"

"I don't know," she replies honestly.

She explains it's possible, but there is no guarantee. I tell her about all of the compensating Gavin is already doing. She is impressed with how he is doing this without being taught. After the diagnosis, she tells me based on her evaluation, Gavin has an above average IQ, which we hope will help him recover. I respect her honesty, explanations, and knowledge about the brain. Before she leaves, she reminds me that kids have the amazing ability to rewire their brains. She is encouraging, which helps offset the news that Gavin may permanently be deaf to words.

Nicole Pierson

We see Dr. Petronio and Dr. Schultz together about ten minutes after she leaves. Dr. Petronio examines his scar and tells me it is healing well. I talk with them about a few clinical trials I found, and Dr. Schultz says she will look into them. I leave the appointment feeling overwhelmed. Gavin is already battling a brain tumor, and has gained nearly twenty pounds in just over a month. We now have added another battle to add to the list. Gavin has loved to talk since he was able. He chats with anyone and everyone. My social butterfly has lost his wings.

We will be home for a week before a third craniotomy. If we can get a lot of the tumor out, Gavin could start to recover from everything and get a break from surgery. I cannot help but wonder what new neurological deficits could show up after another surgery. We know if we stop surgery, he will also suffer neurological consequences and we will lose the fight. It is an impossible situation.

KARISSA IS HERE for our first sign language lesson. She is an American Sign Language interpreter, and has agreed to come one to two times per week to teach us sign language. For this first lesson, I have a list of words written down for her that would be helpful to learn. She patiently teaches us each word, and we all copy her. We mouth the word and do the sign for Gavin. We use pictures if he cannot read our lips. After learning about twenty-five words, we record her on the iPad so we can review later. Gage is too little, although it is cute to see him try. He usually just watches us, attempts to move his hands and arms, before running away to play. Grace amazes me. She is learning every one quickly and then going over to

Gavin to practice. She misses her best friend and is thrilled that she may get to talk to him again.

Gavin is learning fast too. Even with Joe Bully taking over his brain, he picks up sign language easily. After a couple sessions, we have learned about seventy words. I continue to pray after the next surgery, with pressure off the temporal lobe and thalamus, Gavin will slowly understand words again. For now, we are finding a way around it.

I use our new tool to tell Gavin he has to go back. It is both convenient, and harrowing.

"Tomorrow. Go. Hospital," I sign.

"Are we going to get all of Joe Bully this time?" he asks.

"I hope," I mouth.

"God please keep me safe tomorrow and help us get rid of Joe Bully," he says softly as he climbs into bed. I tuck him in and pray too.

"God, you heard the doctors and you know my heart. Tell me what I can do to save him! Tell me, and I will do it," I beg.

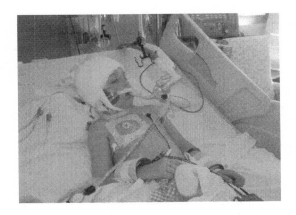

Gavin after his second craniotomy, still sedated and on a ventilator. July 2012.

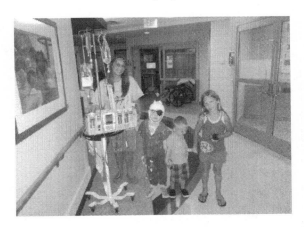

Gavin walking around the PICU at St. Paul Children's with Mom, Grace, and Gage. Summer 2012.

Be Strong and Brave

Chapter Eleven

The pain that you've been feeling,
can't compare to the joy that's coming.

Romans 8:18.

4:00 A.M. COMES fast. It was barely worth it to go to sleep just a few hours ago. Once again, I couldn't sleep and struggled with what I know and what I believe in my heart. I know what the medical journals say, and I know that it appears Gavin will die because of the bully in his brain. Gavin's will to live tells me different. Without this, we would stop. Stop surgeries and pokes and suffering. As painful as it would be, if he was done fighting, I would give him to God.

Nobody has survived this before, but, that does not mean nobody can. For now, we have brain surgery and some possible treatments to try. Gavin does not want to give up. His faith—not given by myself or Steve—but rather by God Himself, is that he will make it. That he will somehow win against Joe Bully, even though it has not been done before.

Nicole Pierson

Gavin has lost the ability to communicate, takes medications all day to balance his brain and body, and would not survive without brain surgery every few weeks, yet he believes he will make it. Not knowing how in the hell that's going to happen, we follow him.

As we walk downstairs, Gavin is still waking up and steroids are making him think he is starving. His eyes light up when he asks, "Can I have breakfast?" The look on my face tells him no. His face goes from light to dim, because he does not remember where we have to go, and why he can't eat.

"Where are we going again?" he asks, as Steve puts his shoes on.

By making a cross on my left bicep, he knows.

Hospital.

His head bowed, he walks towards the garage door without another word. I wish I could say more than my limited sign language. I would explain we are doing surgery to keep the tumor at bay. I wish I could tell him that I research every night looking for a cure, and that I would do anything to save him. I don't know enough sign language to tell him these things, so we drive silently to Children's Hospital instead.

TODAY IS MY anniversary. Steve and I were married ten years ago on August 2, 2002. We had planned to go on vacation to celebrate, but that was before Gavin was sick. We make the best of it, glad the updates have been uneventful. I try to remember what it feels like when I planned our vacation many months ago. I vaguely remember what it was like to get excited about things. It's been so long.

Our biggest hope for today is that more pressure can be lifted off critical areas of Gavin's brain. We hope after this

Be Strong and Brave

surgery, Gavin can have a break and be a boy for a while. I think back to our conversation at the meeting, about surgery possibly giving Gavin years. I wonder what happens if he doesn't get years, but I already know. These surgeries are life-saving measures, not cures.

For now, we have brain surgery and hope. We hope that keeping him alive now is for something more than pointless suffering, and that someday, Gavin can recover from all of the deficits. Although he is only expected to get years, we hope to give him a lifetime.

After another long surgery, Dr. Petronio closes around 11:00 p.m. Unfortunately, Joe Bully is not gone, and the hours of fighting were not enough. Gavin did very well in surgery, except for needing a transfusion for a small amount of blood loss. Some of the tumor was removed off the left side of his brain, and now, the all too familiar road to recovery has begun.

His cheeks are puffy as he sleeps, the ventilator taking his breaths once again. Walking into the intensive care unit feels less scary each time we have to do it. We somberly walk in and get situated for another long stay. Gavin's surgery today was another marathon, and it is now after midnight.

As we wait for him to wake up from sedation, I am nervous about new issues. Will he wake up not able to speak, or see, or walk? Gavin has been lucky to not have any post-op bleeding or swelling thus far, but it's always a real possibility. Last time, he woke up not being able to understand us. Anything is possible in brain surgery, which is why we need better treatments and cures. I dream of a day when the treatment for brain tumors does not alter the patient's entire life, often permanently. It is why I spend every minute possible looking for a cure.

TODAY HAS BEEN hard. I am frustrated, and my soul is lost and unsteady. My dreams of Gavin turning seven, going back to school, and graduating from high school seem too far away from this reality.

By the afternoon, Gavin begins the wake-up process as I lie in bed with him, cuddling around the IV lines. I imagine a day without them. I focus on whatever I can right now that I can control. There is talk about taking his G-tube out because he has no problem getting nutrition with the steroids. One less tube is a small victory. I'll take it.

This morning, he was weighed. He has nearly doubled his weight since starting steroids almost two months ago. Although I have seen this transformation slowly, I can barely recognize him anymore. Since he woke, he has been forgetting things that happened minutes ago, and has been confusing names of people and objects. I tried to ignore the first few mistakes. After all, he just had brain surgery and maybe he's still feeling the effects of the sedation drugs. I know better, but for now I will pretend it's not a thing. Until it's undeniable and I have to face the aftermath of brain surgery once again.

"Hi Grandma!" Gavin says to my sister Missy as she walks into the room. She smiles at him, not caring what he calls her. A few seconds later, he starts to cry because he knows she's not Grandma but he cannot remember her name.

"I'm so sorry I didn't mean to say that," he says apologetically.

She just kisses his forehead and tells him it's okay, wishing she could help him by telling him her name. But she knows he wouldn't hear her, as he did not magically get that skill back after this surgery like I had hoped. Finally, as we sit and chat he proudly says, "I remember now, you are Missy!" I can see his brain trying to sort out the new insult.

I thought I had experienced difficult times in my life, but nothing compares to this. It is devastating to watch his memory fade, and abilities decline. I've had to continually shake my head no when he asks me to order him a sandwich because he thinks he's starving, when really he has just eaten five minutes ago, but can't recall doing so. Eating is about the only thing he can do without assistance, and is the only pleasure he truly enjoys these days as moving has become difficult. People who see him must think I am shoving food down his throat, but truly I spend most of the day trying to distract him from it.

I am patient with him, and use our limited sign language to explain why he cannot eat. I do everything short of a back flip. Partly because I can't do a back flip, because honestly I would do that if it helped him understand or remember. I think back to his kindergarten visit with the ice cream treats earlier this year, and how I naively imagined Gavin doing treatment over the summer and being back to school in the fall. School starts in three weeks. There is no way that is happening.

Three craniotomies in seven weeks is too many, but the tumor continues to be relentless. Each surgery, I am watching a little more of my child slip away. I wonder how he will ever get back to the boy he was, and fear he never will. These thoughts come without warning, and suddenly I feel my heart pounding and my palms sweaty as I hold Gavin's. I ask

Nicole Pierson

the nurse to stay with him while I take a shower. I need an escape.

The shower is hot, and makes my body feel something other than numb. A shower allows me to cry, and doesn't want to talk about it. I try not to cry around people because they would feel the need to react, to console, or say something to help me feel better. Their words may be genuine and caring, but unless they are telling me they have found a cure and my son will not die, it won't help. I don't want to put that on them so I have made the conscious decision to save everything for my shower. I write on Caring Bridge because I can write through tears without a reaction, and can read comments when I feel up to it. Each night, I pray myself to sleep and beg God to guide me. To help us find a cure.

Some days I feel as if He's so close I can feel Him. Other days I wonder if He exists at all. I do not have Gavin's faith, but wish I did. Mine is all over the place. In my universe, I want to understand everything, and this is where it gets muddy. Because I can't possibly understand everything, and faith has to take place of that. So I pray a lot, hoping God will forgive me. I am realizing I cannot understand it all, and when I am weak, I can seek for strength.

MY BIGGEST HOPE in the midst of Gavin's new issues as well as continued struggles, is that we have found a promising clinical trial drug. My aunt Lisa and I have been reading about it, and Dr. Schultz as well. I have now read every single study, including the mice studies, and we are going to be asking Pfizer, the pharmaceutical company, about getting on a trial. The drug has worked to stop the growth of mature teratomas, in three adults. One of them even had a decrease in tumor size.

I am not sure how clinical trials work. But it is a chance, and from what I have read, it may be our only chance. The drug, called Palbociclib, is considered a targeted therapy. I have learned that Gavin's tumor likely grows because of a cell signaling mistake in the G1 phase of the cell cycle. Our cells are very smart, but sometimes they get the wrong message. In Gavin's case, cells are being duplicated before being checked, due to an upregulation (cell increase) of a certain cyclin dependent kinase, which is a protein.

It seems complicated and simple at the same time. If the tumor is duplicating cells so Joe Bully has free rein over my child's brain, we need to stop it. The drug can do that.

One plus one equals two right?

Palbociclib is not currently FDA approved. No children have been given the medicine, which is where it gets complicated. I understand what a huge risk it is to give a child a drug not yet approved, but the way I see it, we lose Gavin for sure or we try to save him. Thus, Dr. Schultz has contacted the doctor in charge of an adult trial in Philadelphia.

These days, when I look at Gavin, and don't see the child I gave birth to, or when I hear him call a giraffe a turtle, I look forward, and I hope for a miracle. The pain and fear would swallow me if I let it and I am too stubborn to allow that to happen.

IT'S DAY SIX post craniotomy and we cannot wait to get out of here. This hospital is amazing, but I need to be with my other children. I miss them so deeply and I need to feel some normalcy. I tell the doctor I can learn to care for him at home.

A nurse could teach me how to take blood pressures, I suggest. I know how to administer medicine, check vitals, and watch for neurological symptoms. I may be overzealous trying to convince him, but I am desperate.

This morning, Gavin had his G-tube removed. He has hated it since the beginning. It needed to be cleaned daily and he was very guarded because of it. He is a little sore, but the surgery to remove it was quick.

To be honest, my patience is fading fast. I thought we would get to go home after the procedure, after selling myself as a home nurse. We are told we will go home tomorrow though, and I can feel my skin crawling. Here at the hospital, we are on display. Every time an issue comes up all eyes are on me, expecting a reaction it seems. With so many set-backs, maybe they are waiting for my optimistic attitude to finally diminish. Not that they want it to, but I know kids in Gavin's condition are eventually sent home to die. They see it all the time, so why would this be any different? I feel like I am on the verge of breaking. All patience is gone.

A new occupational therapist walks in to see Gavin, and begins by asking him a few questions. As he stares blankly ahead, she looks confused. Here we go again, I sigh. I have been explaining his "pure word deafness," over and over again to many different people during this hospital stay. It is in his chart, yet people continue to come in and speak to him, expecting a response. It's making me a little crazy!

I hate that he cannot understand what we are saying. It breaks my heart. Now, I have to once again explain he cannot understand words. I feel the frustration building as I do so. It's completely unprofessional. Read the chart, I think to myself. Once I explain what it is, she talks louder and slower. She doesn't get it, and I am done trying. I wonder what she would do if I told her he was blind. Would she just show him easier pictures? He cannot hear you, I want to scream!

Instead, I sit quietly and disengage.

At home, we focus on baby steps once again, and weaning Gavin off some of the medications he took after surgery. He still cannot understand words, yet sometimes I feel like he can. It's not consistent, and it may be wishful thinking. When I test him to determine if he is hearing words again, he fails. I wonder if I will ever have a conversation with him again. He has picked up sign language very quickly and we are doing well talking to each other, albeit in a different manner. It's enough to meet his basic needs, but I worry what it is doing to his will. Why fight to stay in a world you cannot understand?

YESTERDAY, MY NEPHEW was born and we went to the hospital to visit. It dawned on me once we were there, holding this sweet baby, that Gavin wouldn't be able to hear his name. He held his baby cousin and sang to him— "You are my sunshine"—those words get me every time. I was going to be with my sister-in-law, Azra, when she had the baby, but we were still in the hospital.

With the new memory issues after surgery, Gavin's reading ability took a hit. When we get home, I try to write the baby's name but he cannot pronounce it. He can only read words he previously learned. Even letters are tricky, but he usually can recall them. A new deficit we will need to address. I try to think of some way he can learn his cousin's name. He keeps asking, and we keep trying, until finally I have an idea. I grab a picture of my dad, his grandpa Dan. I point to it and he says, "That's Grandpa Dan!" I nod and just mouth "Dan" back to him.

He repeats "Dan." I give him a thumbs up.

Next I write the letter "A" on a white board. He reads it correctly, with the help of the sign. Finally, I point to the board, then the picture. He says, "A – Dan." We are so close.

I show him the picture on my phone that I took of him holding the baby earlier, and point to the baby. Then back to the board and picture of grandpa. "A – Dan," he says. I say, "Yes, Aidan, that's his name," while pointing to the picture. Gavin figures out that the baby's name is Aidan, with an emphasis on "Dan," for now. Success! He learned his new cousin's name.

After the effort it took for such a simple task, I feel discouraged, yet hopeful. It is going to take a long time to help him learn things, but he wants to learn, and he can if I find the right avenue. I make cards with the words we have learned signs for, and on the card is a picture and the word. We review these daily and I say them over and over again, hoping one day he will not need all of the visual cues, and one day he can hear the word again.

It would be so easy—too easy—to give up. Every day is a struggle. A white flag is always hanging nearby brushing us. Yelling loudly, "Surrender!" A voice inside of me though, says, "Fight." I vow to continue on with every ounce of energy I have. The fog seems as if it will never lift. I guess that's why it's called Faith. I never thought we could *do* this life. I didn't think I would be able to find joy while experiencing such deep emotional pain.

Since we have been home, Gavin cannot sleep. The steroids are slowly being weaned, and he is on many other medications to help with pain, avoid seizures, lower blood pressure, and balance electrolytes. Many medications are on board to battle side effects of another, a frustrating realization. Gavin's knees hurt, he wakes up hungry in the middle of the night, and I am checking his blood pressure and heart rate all day and night. Without faith that this will not always be our life, we wouldn't get through it.

THE FIRST DAY of school is here. The day I hoped Gavin would go back to his life the way it was. Grace looks adorable in her black sequined skirt and butterfly shirt. Usually, I am teaching and cannot send the kids off on their first day of school. I am still on family leave though and soak up the time by making breakfast and taking pictures.

Gavin does not walk with her to the bus stop like he did the year before, when he was so excited to start kindergarten. Instead, I have to help him climb into the minivan to drive a block. He doesn't get out when I walk her up to the bus stop. As she jumps out excitedly, he looks at her and then looks to the kids forming a line at the corner. He chooses not to say a word.

I pretend everything is okay as I smile at other moms and dads on the corner. Minutes before, Gavin tried to put his shoes on and got his backpack.

"Mom, can I please go with Grace to school?" he begged. He cannot physically get on the bus without assistance, and has so much recovering to do before he can. I feel like the worst mom on the planet for telling him no, without fully being able to explain why. What I can tell him is limited with our new sign language abilities, and I wonder what he is thinking as we drive down the street.

I sign to him that he will go to school soon too, but it's not enough. He wants to be a normal kid, getting on the school bus. He misses the days he could run to the bus stop and had enough strength to get out of the van by himself. He takes medications every two hours, and needs assistance for nearly everything. He can barely write, and has been trying to work on it at home. He has lost so much and I don't know how he will get it all back.

I watch Grace step onto the bus and am thankful she is healthy. In the very same thought, I am sad Gavin isn't getting on, too. These days, every time I am happy for milestones of my other children, the fact that Gavin can't, steals the joy. I hate that it happens. I want to feel joy for their accomplishments, but it simultaneously causes so much heartache that I push it away.

As Grace's bus pulls away, I drive home on empty.

Chapter Twelve

I have been driven many times upon my knees
by the overwhelming conviction
that I had nowhere else to go.

Abraham Lincoln

EVERY FEW WEEKS, Gavin goes in for a full MRI of the brain and spine. For obvious reasons, we must monitor this bully closely. His port was put in when he began chemo and he was thin. The past few times his port has been accessed, we have been told it is tilted, likely from the weight gain. I am dreading this as we make our way to Children's for another scan.

As we prepare for the first poke, I feel nauseous. I hold Gavin's hand and hope it works the first time.

"Mom, don't let them poke me, STOP!" Gavin screams.

"Just one poke, Buddy," I mouth to him.

He has stopped trusting me because the first poke didn't work. His port seems to be displaced, the nurse tells me. The second nurse struggles as well. And the next.

The fourth nurse is about to try, as I continue to hold Gavin down with all of my strength. How can I do this to my child? His screams are echoing through the unit. I cannot continue to watch him suffer like this but what choice do I have?

"Hold still," the nurse tells him, not realizing he cannot understand what she is saying, and expecting him to continue to take the pain. I wonder how calm she would be if she were poked repeatedly without knowing when the needles will stop coming.

She cannot access the port, and I demand to be done. Seven pokes and four nurses later, Gavin's chest is left sore and red. All of the suffering for nothing. Is that what this is, God? Pointless suffering? I am fuming. I want to take Gavin away.

Far, far away where he can't be hurt.

Gavin must be wondering why his mother would allow this. He must wonder why I didn't save him from the pain. Why can't I save him from all of this? I feel like I have failed at parenting and at keeping him safe. He is so vulnerable to the predator within, destroying him a little at a time. God, there is nothing I can do. You have to help me!

I am left to make more decisions and decide the scan is not happening. I will not hurt him anymore, at least not today. I ask the nurse to call Dr. Schultz so we can figure out what to do. Thankfully, we are able to give him some anxiety medication so he can calm down after such a traumatic experience.

Be Strong and Brave

"I'm so sorry," I say as he catches his breath from crying so long. "We are all done," I sign. He looks at me with his glossy, tired eyes and nods. He is too exhausted to talk, and as minutes go by, he falls asleep. His body still in spasms from all of the screaming.

Dr. Schultz recommends taking out the port and replacing it with a Hickman line. It is a line that is threaded directly to the blood vessels of the heart and comes out of his chest. It would require a lot of care and has risk of infection, but it can be left in for months and would mean no more pokes. Before she finishes telling me the details I ask, "When can we have it done?"

"I am going to do everything in my power to make it happen tomorrow," she explains. She tells me to take Gavin home and we'll do the scan once he has a Hickman line.

As I wait for him to wake up, the nurses leave me alone. I know that was not easy for them and they would prefer not to make a child suffer. I am not angry at them. I am just broken and feel so out of control. I feel as if I am on a carousel of emotional turmoil that never stops. My sweet boy, I wish I could protect you, I whisper softly as he slowly opens his eyes.

The sky is getting dark when we finally drive home. Gavin isn't watching a movie like he usually does. He is staring out the window, and I wonder what he's thinking. We can't chat in the car like we always did, because he can't read my lips while I am driving. And I can't sign when my hands are on the wheel. So we sit in silence, and he stares at this world around him he so badly wants to stay in. I have time to replay the horror of today, his screams piercing my heart.

Nicole Pierson

I am thankful he will not suffer anymore today. There are new issues every day it seems, and I do not know how we will continue to do this. I say that, and in the same thought know if we give up, Joe Bully wins.

At home, it's a quiet night for all of us. Dr. Schultz calls to let me know Gavin is scheduled for surgery tomorrow morning. I am thankful she was able to get this done. One more poke tomorrow, so he can have sedation medicine.

After that, no more pokes. No more suffering.

GAVIN WAKES UP from surgery and we show him the new tube coming out of his chest. "No more pokes," I say as I hold the line in my hand. He smiles, which is something he hasn't done for days. Up next is the scan we were supposed to do yesterday.

We head to Radiology for the scan and then wait for results. The hospital waiting area continues to be a source of anxiety. I replay the night of the diagnosis, when Gavin confidently walked around. It was the last time I saw him that way. We are called back to the neurosurgery clinic, and Gavin is weighed. He continues to gain weight and hasn't grown in months. I ignore it, so I can stay focused on the results—the words that may admit us, or may allow us reprieve. We are at the mercy of this bully and I hate it!

"The tumor is stable," Dr. Petronio explains. Gavin's ventricles appear to be slightly larger so we are told to keep a close eye on him. We get a couple of low key days at home. Boring, normal days that allow us to breathe. Steve and I finally get out for a date night after months, something I desperately needed.

We went to dinner close by, just in case. My parents came over to watch the kids. Before I left, I prepared all of Gavin's medications on the counter. Grace knows how to help him take the meds, and Gage will hold his hand when his Hickman gets flushed. As I sit across from my husband, I am in awe we are doing this. That we have juggled this life of hospitals and the twenty-four-hour care Gavin needs. For a moment, I forget we are fighting for our child's life. I stare into his eyes as if I am seeing him for the first time in months. Our time away was short, but enough to remind us that although our relationship has been on hold, we are still in this marriage. Right now, we have to keep fighting.

"MY HEAD!" GAVIN screams. I jump up, still half asleep, not sure at this point if I am dreaming or awake. I rush over to him and turn the lamp on.

"Where?" I sign to him. Steve is up too, and we are trying to assess where the pain is coming from.

He holds the back of his head with both hands and says "Here, everywhere on the back of my head," with tears rolling down his face.

I sign to him, "Mom. Go. Get. Medicine," and run so fast down the stairs that I nearly fall, skipping the last step. Lights, I think to myself, they would be helpful. I feel the wall and flip the switches until the kitchen light appears. I pull down a few bottles of medicine and find Oxycodone right away. It says I can give up to four milliliters for severe pain, and I fill the syringe to the max. Within about fifteen seconds, I am running back upstairs.

I give him oxycodone and then I sit on the futon, which is now where he sleeps in our room. I hug him as he cries, and tell him the medicine will be working soon, knowing it will take at least twenty minutes. For a second, he calms down enough to speak.

"Mom, I am sad I have a brain tumor, and it's really hard to live with Joe Bully," he says as I lay his head on my lap. I have nodded to Steve to get some sleep, as he needs to be up for work in two hours. I hold Gavin as we wait for the magic of oxycodone to work.

I manage to use my foot to slide my cell phone across the floor from my bed. I search for Gavin's playlist we made for him in the hospital. Yiruma, a Japanese pianist, begins to play. As I sit here broken and empty, I press play and "River Flows in You," begins. Gavin's tears slowly dry, and his breaths become steady, telling me the pain is slowly leaving. We sit in the darkness, letting the song calm Gavin's anxiety. The song remains on repeat as I hold him. Finally, he is asleep and pain free.

I don't see how this will get better. Lately, we seem to be heading downhill fast. We keep trying to gain our bearings and have some control, but it's not enough.

I know I must call Neurosurgery and let them know about the new headaches. I fear there is too much pressure in Gavin's brain. My chest feels heavy and I am in need of a full breath as I think through the possibilities. After carefully setting Gavin's head on his pillow, I walk around the house in the dark, hoping to distract my mind enough to be able to breathe normally again. Every time I attempt to fill my lungs with air, they constrict. I stop in front of Gavin's preschool picture in the living room. The one with his spiked blonde hair and adorable outfit Auntie Katie put on him.

Katie is one of my three sisters. She was our nanny for a couple of years after Gage was born. My kids love her and she was like their second mom for a while. One of her many talents was making them look adorable. Picture Day was no exception. Gavin looked perfect. I trace the lines of his smile and chin. Lines that are no longer there because of steroids.

Even though looking at this picture is emotional, I distracted my mind enough and finally have steady breaths. I tell myself that no matter what, we have to keep going. I have to keep pushing forward. I feel crippled at the thought of losing him. Before climbing back into bed, I make the dreaded call to Neurosurgery. Increase steroids, it is. A fix for now.

The next couple of days are filled with more hunger and less headaches. Tomorrow Gavin has an MRI to look at the bully and see Neurosurgery. I reluctantly consider the headaches he keeps having, and know there's likely fluid building up in his ventricles again. What we have been trying to avoid all summer seems imminent. A shunt would drain fluid from his ventricles to his abdomen. Another surgery, and another scar on my beautiful boy's head.

We decide to do a limited MRI scan, to look at Gavin's ventricles. Our appointment is Friday morning in St. Paul. Over the next two days, I am to look for signs that I should bring him in sooner. Lethargy, vomiting, confusion, severe dizziness, and headaches. Slowly, the symptoms are worsening, but we manage to hold off rushing him to the ER until his appointment. After the nurse checks us in and takes vitals, Gavin sits with me quietly. He has just done the quick MRI, which takes about twenty minutes.

A KNOCK AT the door is followed by Dr. Petronio's voice. I manage to feel both relief and anxiety. I want Gavin to feel better, but know what that may mean. We could have had the shunt put in from the beginning, but I had naively hoped the tumor would be gone by now, and we could avoid it altogether. Getting one now feels like a giant step in the wrong direction.

"How frequent are the headaches?" Dr. Petronio asks, as he feels Gavin's head.

"Well, I would say for the past week or so, he has a headache all the time unless he has Tylenol or oxycodone," I reply. I really couldn't think of the last time Gavin did not have a headache. As he further examines Gavin, I add, "He seems really tired lately too, and his naps are longer each day."

"Hmmm, okay," Dr. Petronio replies. He is in deep thought, something he does when he has to make hard decisions. After a minute, he says, "Well, I'm afraid the fluid continues to build up and the scans show an increase in ventricles. I think it's best to schedule surgery to insert a shunt for Monday."

I nod, and am thankful there is something to do to take Gavin's pain away.

"I may need to insert two shunts," he continues. "The fluid is also building in the subdural space, likely because of recent surgeries." I continue to nod, trusting every word. Dr. Petronio tells me he is assisting with another brain surgery this afternoon and has reservations about sending us home over the weekend.

"I think if I sent him home, you may be back this weekend, and on very different circumstances, so I think it's best that Gavin is admitted so we can watch him closely."

"Yes, I agree," I say. My intuitions match his. I do not want to bring Gavin back in an ambulance. My mind wonders what he means by "very different circumstances," but I decide I cannot go there right now. The plan is to give Gavin a medication that reduces fluid production in the ventricles, so that he can get through the weekend and have surgery on Monday. We wait for the floor to have an available room. Too many kids are sick, a saddening reality, so it takes a while.

AS WE MAKE our way to the floor, we see familiar nurses and it brings a tiny bit of comfort. They know we spent much of our summer here and if we are back, it's not good. When we finally get settled in, it is about 3:00 p.m. My friend, Jill, is on her way with her children, Louisa and Ty. Gavin met Louisa a few months ago at a play that my other friend Denise took him to. Since then, Louisa has visited him during chemo and other hospital stays. They both have such sweet souls.

I tell Gavin that Louisa is coming and he smiles. He is good at lip reading her name, and I use sign language to help. Soon after I tell him though, he falls asleep. I let him sleep because after all, he did not sleep much last night and the hospital just isn't that exciting so he might as well. Also, we had given him pain medication so he is comfortable. It seemed normal for him to want a nap.

When Jill, her husband Eric, and children arrive, I try to wake Gavin. He does not wake up. Once in a while he opens his eyes but then immediately falls back asleep. The nurse comes in during our visit and begins to ask questions and show concern that he is sleeping. Louisa even sits next to him, touches his face and calls his name. He doesn't respond, and I too, am worried.

Nicole Pierson

After Jill and her family leave, I decide to try a little harder to wake him. I raise his arm up, and loudly say his name. Again, he would open his eyes but they looked very tired and he just could not stay awake. We decide to have a doctor look at him. It's not good.

Gavin needs surgery. He is slipping into a coma because there is too much pressure in his brain. This must have been what Dr. Petronio meant when he talked about different circumstances bringing us in.

More people begin to fill the room. "Hello, I am an on-call anesthesiologist and Dr. Petronio is on his way," an older doctor explains as he comes into the tiny room. Behind him, four other people follow and suddenly I feel like I am watching from another place. They all begin to talk, seemingly at once, and I listen quietly. I do not know any of these people and my anxiety is through the roof. They leave us alone until we can head to surgery. Steve and I sit next to Gavin, who will not wake up at all anymore.

We are quiet, Gavin laying still in the bed next to us. The only noise is the deafening sound of the machines. Finally, I manage some words, "I feel like we are going to lose him!"

"Nicole. Stop. We cannot think like that. Just focus on right now, focus on me." he says, demanding my eyes to meet his.

He is the only person who has the right to tell me to stop worrying. As Gavin's parent, he is the only other person who understands this level of pain, and I know he is right. We have to stay strong, and cannot think we are losing.

Relief sets in us as Dr. Petronio walks into the room. After we tell him about the evening, he tells us he has to attempt to wake him, and that it may not be pleasant.

"Gavin!" he says loudly. Nothing.

While shaking him a little bit, "Gavin!" a little louder. No response.

He attempts stimulation, which is a pinch of pain that people are supposed to wake up to. Gavin lays still. Dr. Petronio knows exactly what he needs to do.

We talk about the surgery and sign the forms again. The ones with all of the possible complications we try to overlook. We know brain surgery is complicated, but it's also the only way our child gets to keep living. Steve and I do not go back to the OR, because he is already in a deep sleep. We make our way to the surgery waiting area and it is now 11:30 pm.

Wake up Gavin, I plead. I promise, we will keep fighting for you.

Chapter Thirteen

If you're going through hell, keep going.
Never, never, never give up.

Winston Churchill

THE WAITING AREA is dark and still as we wait. Suddenly the phone rings forcing me to be alert.

"Hello?" I say with concern in my voice.

The nurse on the line is calm. "Gavin is doing fine. Dr. Petronio has finished with the ventricular shunt and is working on a subdural shunt which should take about an hour."

"Okay, we will move up to the PICU waiting room and wait there," I reply. I hang up and we gather our things to head upstairs.

As they wheel Gavin past us in the waiting area, a nurse finds my fearful eyes. She does not say a word as they wait for the intensive care unit doors to be opened. Her soul tells mine that she wishes this wasn't Gavin's life. That she wishes he could catch a break. She covers Gavin's tubes and

Be Strong and Brave

lines with his blanket, before pushing him through the PICU doors.

I am guessing she was called from home, at 10:00 p.m., to come in and assist with this emergency surgery. Maybe she was with her children, enjoying a Friday night movie, or maybe she was finally relaxing after a busy week. I am so thankful for this team and their commitment to those in need, who give up Friday nights so that a child might wake up.

When we see Gavin, he is on a ventilator, which is familiar. So much that it doesn't startle me as it has before. I am like a zombie as I walk in and prepare for a few hours of sleep. It is now close to 3:00 a.m. I kiss Gavin's cheek and fall to the bed.

Seven a.m. comes quickly. Steve is up, talking to the intensivist who is telling him the plan for today. I want to keep sleeping and get a few more hours of a break from reality. But Gavin will soon be extubated (the breathing tube will be removed), so I hop up and decide to take a quick shower.

HIS FIRST WORDS after an emergency brain surgery remind us how amazingly compassionate he is.

"Dad, is someone watching Grace and Gage? I'm worried about them," he says in his post ventilator voice. This kid. He cares so much, loves so much, and deserves so much more than this.

"Yes Buddy, don't worry. They are with Grandma and Grandpa Marshall," Steve assures.

Late morning, the Neurosurgery nurse practitioner Julie, stops by and checks on Gavin. Everything seems to be working as expected, and the new shunts should decrease pressure enough to stop steroids. Julie unwraps Gavin's bandage slowly, and what looks like horns, protrude from Gavin's skull. I ask Julie if she thinks they will be permanent and she says maybe not the subdural shunt, but once a ventricular shunt is placed, Dr. Petronio does not usually remove them. Gavin's appearance had already changed so drastically over the past two months. Now his head, full of scars and bald, has two devices he may always need, and which could malfunction, requiring additional surgery. Devices that mean we are getting further from a cure.

I email Dr. Schultz about the status of Pfizer possibly allowing a trial for pediatric patients to take their drug. She gets back to me quickly, and I hear what I don't want to. They are not ready to start a pediatric trial. Maybe next year, they tell her. Next year? We may not have that much time. A fourth craniotomy may not be enough to stop this bully from invading, destroying, and taking more of my child away with its power.

AT HOME, GAVIN'S headaches disappear. It is a much needed break. We are weaning steroids as well, so his appetite decreases. The plan is to stay out of the hospital and give him some time to be six. With the news about not getting on a trial with Pfizer, we talk about more surgery.

The tumor was stable the last time we scanned. It seemed to stop growing for now. Our hope is enough tumor was taken out, and cauterized, for the growth to be stopped, or at least slowed. Surgery continues to be our only weapon, and we will be using it again for a fourth craniotomy sooner than we would like.

We need to make it to next year.

As GRACE WALKS by, I notice she has tears in her eyes. "What's wrong sweetie?" I ask as I motion for her to sit on my lap. She is holding a picture of her and Gavin from when they were four and five. She stares at it nostalgically while sitting down.

"When will I get my brother back?" she cries.

"Oh sweetie, I know it's hard," I say, struggling to find the right words.

Of course, I have realized how much Gavin's illness has interrupted her life, but I haven't had much time to stop and think about their relationship and how drastically it had changed. They were best friends. She too, has watched Gavin transform into a different brother.

"I just want Joe Bully gone so Gavin can be back to normal again," she continues.

I take a deep breath while I hug her tight and try to think of some kind of reaction. The truth is, he may not ever get back to normal, if he survives. The truth is that he may die from this bully inside his head. The truth is too painful, too burdensome for a seven-year-old.

"Grace, we are all working to save Gavin. His doctors, Mom and Dad, everyone, wants Gavin to get better," I say as I wipe her tears. She looks up at me with hope.

"Gavin isn't on steroids anymore, and hopefully he will have some time to get better now that he has shunts. Maybe he will even want to play outside again," I offer, desperately wanting to believe it.

"Yeah, maybe he could run again and climb the stairs in the playhouse," she says, trying to imagine it.

"Just pray to God when you feel this way, and He will be there for you. Grace, I believe that He visited Gavin for a reason, and I know it's tough, but we just have to keep going." Saying this out loud reminds me to believe it.

"Okay, Mom," she says, while she hangs up her backpack and picks Gage up from the floor. At three, he has become her new playmate. He too, has experienced too much.

EVERY MORNING ONCE Grace goes to school, the boys and I either do activities together at home or venture out. Today, we are going to the library to get some more books for Gavin. Although he struggles to figure out what the words on the page mean, I am determined to keep trying.

"Come on, Gage, we are going to go to the library and get some books!" I say as I grab his shoes and motion for him to sit on the stairs. As he sits down, Gavin rushes into the living room. I haven't seen him move this fast in months.

"Mom!" He shouts excitedly, "I heard you say library!"

There is no way he could have seen our lips, which would have been his only way besides sign language to understand what we are saying. He was two rooms away, around the corner.

"You heard me say library?" I clarify, using sign language.

"Yes, Mom. I heard you say that we are going to the library," he tells me again with confidence.

Tears begin to stream down my face before I even know what emotion I am feeling. I hug Gavin and feel goose bumps on my right bicep. God immediately enters my mind. Maybe He was not actually touching my arm—but as I sit here realizing Gavin's brain is rewiring, I feel as if this miracle is a glimpse of something more.

The neuropsychologist told us Gavin may never hear words again. But he is, with a large tumor in the center of his brain, and after three invasive craniotomies. What else is Gavin capable of?

Over the next few days, I would occasionally test Gavin by having him close his eyes, as I slowly said a word. I started with words we had learned signs for. I would say it, and he would repeat it. Without sign language or any visual cues he was repeating them. I think because we always said the word and signed it, he was relearning what sounds match what words. "Library" was one of the signs he knew and was what began this realization that Gavin is beating odds once again. We did not have a way to beat Joe Bully, but Gavin's amazing brain is fighting back. He heard me, and found a way around the bully. His resilience and determination to do this gives me hope that one day, he will be cured.

I MADE PLANS to go back to work in November. I carry the health insurance, and am now paying out of pocket, a much higher rate because I am out of paid time off. Steve and I are going to switch roles, though I hate the thought of leaving Gavin. As if I wasn't already beginning to have anxiety about the change, Gavin began to show symptoms of another complication.

"Mom, is blue the tree on there?" Gavin asks as he opens his eyes.

"What Gavin?" I ask, confused.

"Over there, in my head," he points to nothing.

He is slurring and the words that are coming out are not the ones he intended.

Nicole Pierson

While holding his left eye, he says "Ouch!" Yesterday, he complained that his eye hurt and his head a little. He fell asleep early, and seemed off. Now his words do not make sense and it seems there is pressure despite the shunts. I don't even call, we just get in the car and head to Children's Hospital. As we approach the registration window, we mention brain tumor, confusion, and dizziness to the ER nurse and she brings us right back. He was fine, and now he's not, becoming more lethargic, telling me there has to be pressure somewhere. As we wait to be seen, Gavin falls asleep and seems completely exhausted. So much that he will only open his eyes for a moment before dozing off again.

A CT scan shows slightly enlarged ventricles, and Gavin is admitted to the PICU once again. Thinking it's related to the new shunts, Dr. Petronio taps his VP shunt to release some fluid. Gavin perks up within a few minutes. He wakes up to say one sentence.

"Dr. Petronio, I didn't like it when you said I had a beer belly," Gavin says sarcastically.

The room of worried doctors, nurses and parents, explodes in laughter. About a month ago, joking of course, Dr. Petronio and Gavin were discussing Buffalo Wild Wings and all of the other things Gavin craved on steroids. Despite short term memory deficits at the moment, and having pressure on his brain, Gavin managed to get a room full of people smiling.

Overnight, Gavin wakes up a couple of times but seems peaceful. He is being monitored for any changes in neurological status. The team thinks it could be a shunt malfunction. Unfortunately, shunts have a high rate of both malfunction and infection.

Be Strong and Brave

The next morning, the shunt is externalized, which means the end of the shunt is surgically taken out. We can observe how much fluid it is draining to be sure the shunt is working properly. Gavin's tummy is the exit site, so we have to be very careful around him, even when moving blankets or IV lines. He is more alert today and not as confused as he was yesterday. If today's MRI shows a decrease in ventricles, we can assume that the scary stuff yesterday was in fact a malfunction. If so, Gavin will have a fourth craniotomy tomorrow morning and the shunt will be internalized and fixed if needed. We decide to sedate him for the MRI because it will be a long one of the brain and spine, as well as a few new scans to rule out additional issues.

AS WE WAIT for results, we try not to worry. Gavin is enjoying the new *Madagascar* movie and visiting with my sisters, Katie and Laura, when Dr. Petronio comes in to tell us what is going on.

"I'm afraid I have some bad news," he says straight away. I lean in closer, wishing I could press pause to prepare for whatever he's about to say, but he continues.

"Gavin has a quarter-size blood clot in his brain, at the back of his head in the transverse sinus," Dr. Petronio continues with reluctance.

A blood clot in his brain. God, no.

No surgery tomorrow. IV heparin. Stay awhile. Tests and more tests. All of the words whirl around me like leaves in the fall.

There are serious risks. With heparin and the shunt externalized, we can control pressures. The bigger problem is if the clot broke off and traveled, causing a pulmonary embolism, which can be fatal. God, I don't understand. Gavin is being strong and brave. Where are you?

The craniotomy is officially on hold so we can deal with yet another complication. Before the night is over, Gavin gets hooked up to IV heparin, a blood thinner. I imagine the clot from Gavin's brain, traveling down past his jugular vein, to his heart, resulting in a catastrophe.

THIS MORNING I find myself relieved that Gavin is in the intensive care unit with a blood clot in his brain. Although a blood clot is scary, he wasn't the child next door who just coded. As I walk out of Gavin's room, with my sister-in-law, Azra, we are shoved out of the way. A crash cart and a team of nurses and doctors are rushing into room six. I glance in to see a doctor on the bed, giving chest compressions. I say a silent prayer that God does not take this boy from his family. As we exit the double doors, we look to the waiting area. His family fills the room.

We do not make eye contact and keep walking.

I know it's not normal to feel like my child is okay because he isn't coding. I am to the point of desperation though, of giving up. The truth is, Gavin could code too, and there is nothing I can do to stop it.

Azra and I shake our heads as we replay what we just saw. She encourages me, saying that at least I was able to get Gavin here, and they are treating this clot. I agree and focus on that. As we eat lunch, I notice how crazy the fog is outside. Its thickness is vast and heavy, much like my heart.

"Yeah, Matt was driving like twenty miles per hour on the highway because we couldn't see," she tries, hoping to distract me for a few minutes. Fighting a brain tumor is like being in a constant fog. It is difficult to know where we are going these days. It's like we can only plan for what is right in front of us, and cannot see beyond that. Every time we try, a life-threatening condition appears without warning. If I squint, I can almost see a different life, and hope for what is there. Someday, maybe the fog will lift and blue skies will be abundant. Somewhere over the rainbow, right?

At the end of the school year, Gavin's teacher made a DVD and gave a copy to Gavin when she brought his diploma. She warned me that there may be tears. As soon as she left, I watched my boy grow and learn with a smile on his face. His nervous, first-day-of-school smile, transformed to a confident boy measuring objects and reading books on the mat. Pictures from the fall field trip flash on the screen. My favorite was when the firefighter threw Gavin over his shoulder and Gavin's smile told it all. Images of a carefree, confident child continued as the song "Over the Rainbow" played. It was the version by Israel Kamakawiwo'ole and it intertwines "What a Wonderful World" as well.

His voice is full of promise, while his string guitar is calm. The words resonate with me. Gavin could be that boy in the video again. I know it doesn't look as he ever will, but if we are going to continue to fight, I have to believe it's possible.

After we eat, we find our way back to the PICU, where things have calmed down. Thankfully, the boy who coded, is still in room six. I am relieved when I see his family heading to see him. I walk into Gavin's room, and he is joking with Steve. He appears less confused which I hope means the clot is not worsening.

Nicole Pierson

OVER THE NEXT couple of days Gavin is getting up and feeling better. He no longer confuses words or talks gibberish. Thankfully, the blood clot has been stable as they monitor with scans, allowing us to switch from IV blood thinners to subcutaneous injections. They have inserted a catheter in his arm, which can be used to inject the medicine. Rather than getting two pokes a day, he will need this catheter port changed weekly. Once it is determined that the dosing is correct with the injections, we are on our way home.

At home, a longer medication list threatens to push me over the edge. There are so many medications and cares Gavin needs. It requires much mental effort and energy. It reminds me of having a newborn. A new surgery date is on the calendar, giving us a couple of weeks out of the hospital. After finally getting off of steroids, the clot and pressure were reason to restart. We are tapering his dose once again, and this time he is on a lower strength steroid, making him very emotional. Today, he tried to read an easy book he could read in kindergarten. He struggled with words he once knew, and looked at me for answers.

"Mom, everything looks weird," he says waiting for me to tell him it was a trick. It was like I gave him a book with words all over the page, or squished on top of one another, and made no sense.

I point to the word "look"—a word he knew well. He stares at it long and purposeful but cannot read it. He knows it is four letters. He guesses, "Down?"

"No Gav, it's look," I sign. Although Gavin can hear words when spoken slowly and he can repeat them, we still heavily rely on sign language.

He shuts the book and walks away with frustration. These days, he cannot walk fast, but he is almost running. With no further to go he gets to the family room and turns around, holding his head with both hands, sobbing. He wants his life back. I want to break down with him, just cry and yell and throw something. Instead, I carefully walk over and sit next to him.

I sign to him.

"Gavin, you are smart. Joe Bully is making things hard. Mom will help you though."

We take deep breaths together and the anxiety slowly dissipates. I realize Gavin cannot read or even recognize letters anymore. He was just doing this a few weeks ago. What happened? There are so many moving parts—tumor, fluid, shunts, blood clot—that it's hard to know.

That rainbow is so far away.

When I think about the next few months, I fear growth of the tumor. I fear brain damage from continued surgeries. I fear Pfizer won't give us the medicine and I will have to bury my child. These are my everyday fears. Each day, I try to give my fear to God. I am not always successful.

AS WE PULL into the red ramp at Children's Hospital for another brain surgery, my stomach turns. I open Gavin's door and he doesn't budge. Looking straight ahead he signs.

"I. Want. Go. Home."

"Sorry. Hospital. Joe Bully. Gone." I sign in return.

Right now, surgery is all we have, our only choice. He bravely gets out of the car and walks with us into the surgery center.

Nicole Pierson

I feel like it's Groundhogs Day. Stable, blood transfusion, scan, PICU. Keep him sedated overnight and do a post-op scan in the morning before waking him up. I could be a spokesperson for craniotomies, unfortunately.

Gavin has never had trouble with the process of getting the ventilator out. This time however, as they remove it, his oxygen levels plummet. Nobody knows why he is having trouble. We determine that maybe he just needs more time, and decide to try again later. Gavin wakes up during the second attempt and looks for us. Steve and I stand in his line of sight as his hand shakily moves towards his face.

"Soon," he signs as he brings his fingers to his chin, pinching his index to his thumb. He can't breathe, but he can sign. We will take what we can get.

"Yes Buddy, we will take the tube out soon." I say, hoping it's true. "Soon. Out." I simplify. My God, my heart is breaking. He cannot continue to go through brain surgery!

He patiently shows his understanding by squeezing my hand, and decides he might as well sleep if he cannot eat, something he hasn't done for about thirty hours now.

Someday, the fog will lift, and he will breathe easily. Someday, he will spend more time out of the hospital than in it. Somewhere, after so many dark clouds, maybe we will find a rainbow.

Chapter Fourteen

HOPE is putting faith to work
when doubting would be easier.

Thomas S. Monson

I FEEL REMORSEFUL as I wake up to the team of medical staff
in the room. Guilt because I slept, while Gavin sat hungry with
a tube in his throat. Last night, I had one of the best nights of
sleep while in the hospital. I didn't dream, and had hours of
uninterrupted rest that's nearly unheard of here. I think about
how dry and raw Gavin's throat is. I know I need sleep, water,
and food. People ask me if I am taking care of myself. Don't
they realize I am not the one dying? I get it, from an outsider's
perspective. It's healthy to get a break from the stress of
parenting a child with a life-threatening disease. Knowing this,
I have tried. Really, I have.

It hasn't worked yet.

Last week, I went running after someone told me it
had helped them during a hard time in their life. As my chest
tightened and my calves warmed, it felt amazing. The wind in

my hair and quickness of my feet felt like I was getting somewhere for once. We have been fighting to move forward, but are lucky to stay in the same place. I pictured Gavin running as he often did. I remembered the day we bought him cleats for baseball. He would put them on and run in the yard. He would come in and exclaim he was as fast as lightning!

I felt good, on top of the world, actually. Each step seemed effortless, which is a rare occasion for me while running. My steps began to slow as my mind raced. Suddenly, the tightness of my chest came back, the feeling that I couldn't take a full breath. I panicked as Gavin's future played out, like a movie in my mind. I knew at that moment, I needed to do something more than run. Running won't save him. I turned towards home, now sobbing. I've tried to do things for myself, but each time I do, I find myself wanting to be by Gavin, or searching for a cure.

I WALK OVER to Gavin, hoping he has been breathing better overnight. I am guessing he is doing well, or I would have been woken up from my slumber. My baby who grew inside of me, please catch your breath. I promise if you do, so will I.

"For every thirteen breaths, Gavin is taking eight on his own," the respiratory therapist says.

"Is that a good thing?" I ask, concerned.

"Yes. Yesterday he was only taking a couple and the machine was doing most of the work. He is getting stronger and we will continue respiratory treatments today," he explains.

As the medications decrease, Gavin is more alert and able to sign to us. He is doing a great job understanding Steve and me, even with his eyes closed. Just to make sure he was

Be Strong and Brave

doing well neurologically, I tell him I am going to show the nurse the picture of Sleeping Beauty kissing him in Disneyworld. He shook his head purposefully, telling me loud and clear, "No!"

Gavin spends the day fighting. Trying to take more and more of his own breaths, and rely less on the ventilator. As we watch the breaths rise and fall on the monitor, we are reminded of how delicate the brain is and how badly we need a cure.

It is excruciating to wait for Gavin to wake up, wondering what new deficits he will have to face. I painfully wonder if we are putting him through all of this unnecessarily. What if these are the last months of his life, spent in a hospital bed? What if his cure will only be in heaven, and we made his life worse trying to save him? I have to work on not knowing, yet still believing. I try to have faith like Gavin that by some miracle, he will be okay. When I'm afraid, I talk with Gavin. He leads me, at six, to trust God and not be afraid. He tells me he will survive.

By the end of the day, Gavin is relying little on the ventilator and there is talk of extubating him tomorrow. Steve and I sleep in shifts, because we want to watch the breaths, and be awake in case they decide to extubate. Three days. That is how long Gavin has had a tube in his throat.

THE RESPIRATORY THERAPISTS and intensivist are here to try to remove his breathing tube again. He has shown enough progress to earn a second attempt. For about twenty minutes, Gavin has been pointing to the tube and signing, "Out." The intensivist hovers over Gavin, and carefully removes the tape that holds the tube in place. Gavin does not like it. I am by his feet, holding them saying, "Okay Gav, we are going to take the tube out, it's almost done." I wince as the tube slowly comes out of his body.

All eyes are on the machine.

Everyone is still and quiet as the machines begin to plummet. Yet they rise again quickly this time. "Saturation is at 88%, a therapist says to the doctor. A few more seconds pass, and Gavin coughs. "96%, I think we are good," he says, as I hold Gavin's hand. Everyone watches a few more minutes to be sure, the intensivist ready to re-intubate if necessary. Gavin tries to speak, but nothing comes out. I grab the green swabs and am ready with a cup of water. He sucks the water out of them as if he's been in a desert for a month. His mouth is extremely dry and I imagine the cold water feels good on his throat. After about ten minutes of that, he finally is able to speak.

"I'm scared of that," he says in a deep raspy voice, with tears streaming down his cheeks. "I know you are, Gav, it's all over," Steve says, while fixing Hoppy's ears which have fallen. I wish this was over for good, and Gavin didn't have to endure all of this just to stay alive.

THE NEXT COUPLE of days are slow. Gavin is not bouncing back like he did with the first three craniotomies. After talking with Neurosurgery, we are told that he was not given as high of a dose of steroids, because we are trying to keep him off of them. The steroids likely helped him bounce back quicker in the past, and now he is doing more of the work on his own.

His body is beginning to feel all that has been done. He is tired and cannot go on like this forever. We are trying to make it to next year, with hopes Gavin can get on a pediatric clinical trial.

A quiet weekend of rest and recovery ends with the news we get to go home. Thankfully, things have been boring. The PICU likes when things are boring, hence our ticket out the door. Despite having had brain surgery just days ago, Gavin walks out of the hospital, with Steve on one side and Travis on the other. I follow behind, in awe of his strength.

OUR TRANSITION TIME is over, and tomorrow I am supposed to go back to work. As a teacher, I am on display for students and need to figure out how to keep it together and teach math, while my child fights for his life. As I prepare to walk out the door, I wonder why I bothered putting on makeup. I have not left Gavin's side for more than a few hours since April. It's a lot like leaving a newborn for the first time. Thankfully, I only work two weeks before Thanksgiving break.

Going back to work brings about new challenges. I am different now, I realize. I try to care about solving for x, but it reminds me there is no equation for curing Gavin. It feels good to get ready each day though, and to be with my coworkers again. As much as I hate to admit it, I did need a break. Work is a break.

I call during every prep and lunch. Gavin loves being with Dad. Steve takes him to physical therapy, oncology and neurosurgery appointments, and follow-up scans. Things are stable for now. Finally, a break Gavin has needed so badly.

"Watch, Mom!" Gavin says excitedly when I walk in the door. He climbs the stairs without stopping. When he gets to the top he is out of breath, but proud.

Nicole Pierson

"Awesome Gav, did you and Dad work on that today?"

"Yeah, and I didn't need any help!" he replies. I realize he didn't ask me to repeat my question.

For the past few weeks, Gavin's pure word deafness has been improving exponentially. It started with repeating one word at a time. Then a couple of words at a time, said very slowly. Today, he can understand most of what is being said to him. Occasionally he asks someone to repeat what they said but relies less on sign language. It is amazing how far he has come. It demonstrates his will to live, to get his life back.

If the tumor can just stop growing for a while, Gavin can have more recovery time. We would have time to get into the trial, or find something else. Dr. Petronio has worked on the tumor for about forty hours, but it still remains. I think many surgeons would have given up by now, knowing the tumor will just keep growing back. All of those hours, and all of the risks. Thankfully, God has given us a surgeon that does not give up easily.

"It is like cement," he once told us after a surgery. The tumor, a teratoma, is made up of all of the same cells the human body is made of. Bone, skin, and organ-like tissues. Some teratomas have been known to have eyeballs, teeth, and hair. Imagine trying to chip away at bone right next to brain tissue. Delicate brain tissue, that controls every personality trait, memory, and physical ability. Dr. Petronio could have given up, he could have seen the future for Gavin unfolding coupled with the hours of difficult surgery. He could have told us there's nothing more he can do. Instead, I believe he also saw something in Gavin that everyone around him seems to notice. His unwavering faith and strength. Gavin was pushing all of us further than we thought possible.

When people ask us how many more surgeries Gavin will need, I want to scream. I know they just want to know. So do I, but we don't get that luxury. We are walking through uncharted territory, the future unknown. I suppose technically, the future is known according to history. The history of this disease says Gavin will eventually die.

Gavin's faith is all we have, as we hope the tumor is done invading. We hope that each surgery is making Joe Bully smaller, and that a cure will be found. That's all we have. Faith and hope. As I create a Christmas card this year, I try to find words that may help family and friends understand where we are at. I wish I could tell them that all of the pain and months in the hospital resulted in Gavin getting his life back, and being tumor free. I don't want the card to be sad either. I come across the perfect quote:

"Faith consists of believing when it is beyond the power of reason to believe." –Voltaire

As an outsider, I know how it looks. It appears we will not be able to keep up, and eventually the tumor will win. When I take a step back, I see it too. But I refuse to accept it. I choose to listen. I listen closely when Gavin speaks of God's words to him. As scared as I am, I follow Gavin, and I follow God.

WITH CHRISTMAS ONLY weeks away, we decide to set up a tree and decorate. It's a normal thing that may help this all feel closer to normal. "Daddy, I want to put the star on the tree!" Grace exclaims. The boys shrug their shoulders as they hang their ornaments on the tree. "Okay baby girl, we will do that last. Why don't you help your brothers spread the ornaments apart?" Steve replies. We watch as they decorate, grabbing more decorations from the Christmas bins. Gavin has lost some weight now that he's off steroids. For a moment, we feel like the battle is over, or at least on pause.

"Gavin, this is your preschool ornament," Grace shows him.

"Oh, I remember this!" Gavin says excitedly. It is a picture of them on Santa's lap, last Christmas. I look at it and cannot believe how much he has changed. In the picture, he has bright, thick, blonde hair. He has that smirk on his face, where one eye is slightly more closed than the other and his smile is there, but trying not to be.

He was so handsome, and his body was free of scars.

"I'm going to put this as high as I can reach!" Gavin says. He reaches up to a spot in need of decorating, and places the ornament. "Perfect!" I tell him.

The days leading up to Christmas, I focus on being present. Having faith, and trusting Gavin and God. Maybe it is the season, but I am in a good place. Christmas Eve has always been a big celebration in my family, so we are heading out to my aunt's house for the evening. As we drive through the snow, I focus on each snowflake, and point out all of the lights on the houses. Gage is thrilled each time more lights come into his line of sight. "Ooooohh," he says every time we drive past. Grace is keeping track of how many houses have white lights, blue lights, or colored lights. With her pen and paper, she is tallying as we go. Gavin is quiet.

GAVIN HASN'T BEEN able to run with the kids for months now, but he usually wants to at least be near them. Tonight, he has stayed close to me, sleeping on the couch and not eating. "Is he feeling okay?" my aunt Lisa asks. I try to explain it away but should know better by now. I discuss medication changes and lack of good rest the night before. "I will probably bring him in soon for a check-up," I conclude. As wrapping paper flies around him, and kids jump excitedly, Gavin sleeps.

At home, Steve and I chat as we stuff stockings and wrap the last few presents for the kids. "Did you notice that Gavin seemed off tonight?" I ask quietly as to not wake them.

"Maybe there was just too much going on," Steve says as he hangs the stockings. "Yeah, I guess," I reply.

"Let's just see how he is tomorrow," he suggests, cleaning up the wrapping paper mess. After what seemed like a minute of sleep, the kids are squealing about.

"Mom, Dad, wake up!" they yell.

"Santa came! He brought presents!" Grace exclaims.

This year, Santa was especially good to the kids. Jam Hops, where all of my kids have done gymnastics, had collected donations and purchased gifts for the kids. Not just a few. The living room was full of gifts. In the middle was a Power Wheels' car for Gage. His eyes lit up and he jumped in the driver seat.

As we watch their eyes widen, we are reminded how blessed we are to have the support we do. With one income and stacks of medical bills, there is no possible way we could have given them a Christmas. We are amazed at the kindness.

Gavin missed a lot this year. Easter, Fourth of July, birthday parties and other celebrations. It's wonderful to watch him this morning. Smiling, opening presents, laughing. His excitement fades fast though, and by 10:00 a.m., he is falling asleep. I decide to make the dreaded call to Neurosurgery.

I dial the on-call line and ask them to page Dr. Petronio. It's Christmas, and there is no way I would be paging him if I didn't think something was wrong. A few minutes later, my cell rings, and I head upstairs where it is quiet.

"Hello?" I answer expectantly.

"Hi. This is Dr. Petronio. Tell me what's going on," he responds, in a concerned voice.

I explain that Gavin has been more tired, his eyes seem to be off, not tracking together, and his pupils are different sizes. I tell him about the morning, how he could only stay awake for a short time.

"Well," he pauses, "Do you think he needs to come in now?"

"No, I think it could wait until tomorrow," I reply. I didn't want to ruin his Christmas, or steal the tiny amount of normalcy we have today for Grace and Gage. He tells me he will have someone call me in the morning about an MRI. Gavin, next to me, asks if he can talk to Dr. Petronio.

"Could Gavin talk to you for a minute?" I ask, realizing this is beyond the duties of a neurosurgeon.

Without hesitation he replies, "Sure."

"Hi Dr. Petronio," Gavin says sweetly. "I just wanted to say Merry Christmas!" Although I couldn't hear his response, Gavin smiled and hung up the phone.

The rest of the night, we watched movies and relaxed. Gavin remained calm and quiet. He took his meds, told us he loved us, and went to sleep. Six weeks. That is how long it's been since he has been out of the hospital. It gave us a taste of what life could be someday, but I fear it's over.

THE NEXT MORNING, we decide not to sedate Gavin for the scan. He brings a movie to watch and falls asleep half way through it. I have sat through these scans enough times to know they usually do not stop a picture half way through. Not when the patient is being still and cooperating as well as Gavin is right now. Suddenly, the noise stops and it's eerily silent.

The door opens, and the tech asks me to step out. Julie, from Neurosurgery, is standing at the doorway. I know by her body language, it is not good news.

"It has grown again," she says. She tells me what I was afraid I already knew.

"Oh my God, what are we going to do?" I cry, hugging her because I don't know what else to do. After four craniotomies, this monster continues to take over Gavin's brain.

We are running out of options faster than we thought.

Nicole Pierson

Gavin on Christmas day 2012

Grace, Gavin, and Gage – January 2013

Be Strong and Brave

Chapter Fifteen

When you come to the end of your rope,
tie a knot and hang on.

Franklin D. Roosevelt

THE WEEKEND WAS quiet. I go back to the articles and case studies I had read multiple times before, thinking maybe I missed something. If I wasn't desperately searching, I was with Gavin.

Tomorrow we meet with Dr. Petronio about what this growth means. We have to talk about the hard reality we have in front of us. I am praying incessantly he can do something, and that this is not the beginning to the end. I am not ready to give up. Gavin is still fighting.

One treatment we talked about a few months ago, while looking into the Palbociclib trial, was Interferon. This drug is FDA approved, but not for teratoma brain tumors. There was a study of another child showing a response, although the teratoma was in another location, not in the brain. This was the medicine we talked about using as a last resort.

So that's where we are, I guess.

In the morning, we will be at Minneapolis Children's Hospital for the Interferon treatment. He will be monitored for a reaction for an hour afterwards. After that, we will head over to St. Paul Children's Hospital to speak with Neurosurgery.

This crept up on us. We knew every surgery was a fight, but when constantly fighting, it's hard to figure out when we began to lose. In boxing, I wonder if the boxers know they are going to lose the fight early on, or if it happens suddenly? Do they think they can still win, even when the blood fills their eyes? I imagine they put all of their strength and endurance into the fight until they are knocked out, or until a winner is declared. We fought every round of this fight, thinking we would win. Even though the opponent had never been beaten before. Even though this tumor had taken lives at this stage of the disease, we thought we had a chance. Underdogs can win, I've seen it.

GAVIN LOOKS FOR Melissa as we walk into Prairie Oak Church. After our encounter at Target, and the outpouring of support of this church, we decided to try it out. We have come a few times and each time we have, everyone is so welcoming. I have never felt that I can actually feel God until we started coming here. When I listen to Pastor Steve speak, I feel Him.

"Melissa!" Gavin yells excitedly, as soon as he spots her. She comes over and he wraps his arms around her to give her a hug. They have only met a few times, but he is so connected to her—so drawn to her kindness.

Be Strong and Brave

"I have something for you," she says. I lean down and help him open the case with a children's Bible inside. There is a bookmark Melissa has placed for him. On this page was the following verse:

"Here is what I am commanding you to do. **Be strong and brave**. Do not be terrified. Do not lose hope. I am the LORD your God. I will be with you everywhere you go." – Joshua 1:9

Gavin excitedly says, "That's what God said to me!" after I read it aloud. The chatter around us seems to leave us still.

"Wow," I say in awe, goosebumps on my right arm once again.

"I know, right?" Melissa continues. "I was flipping through this Bible and landed on that page." I tell her I am going to have to go home and read the story of Joshua.

Bible study wasn't really ever my thing. I did study parts of the Bible when I was in Confirmation classes, but I always felt like I should be making connections that weren't there. I felt inadequate, unable to relate to the words. More than I could have ever imagined, the Bible is speaking to me. To my son, who has been fighting to live long enough for a cure.

Do not lose hope. Do not be terrified.

Okay God, I hear you. I feel calm and trusting as I go about my day. Nothing about Gavin's options have changed, but I have changed. We still have hard conversations tomorrow, and Gavin still has to go through a treatment that may do more harm than good. After dinner, I sit down to read the story of Joshua.

Nicole Pierson

Joshua became a leader after Moses died. God told him to be strong and courageous and to lead the Israelites across the Jordan River to the Promised Land. The Israelites ultimately defeat the Canaanites, and the moral of the story is God will give victory to his people when they obey him. God knew this task would not be easy and that many would doubt it could be done.

I believe it is no coincidence that Melissa found this and gave the Bible to Gavin today. It's a children's version, which is why the wording is slightly different. So, hold on… let me get this straight. God came to Gavin. He commanded him to be strong and brave, just as He told Joshua.

I have to admit, I selfishly believed God came to Gavin to heal him. I was hoping for a miracle. But every time Gavin came out of surgery with a mass still in his brain, I lost that belief. Every complication, my faith was challenged. Could it be that this journey is not about an easy miracle, but rather about not losing hope? Maybe it's about not giving in to fear, for something bigger than we even can imagine.

DR. SCHULTZ WAS contacting Pfizer again to ask about the medicine. They told us "next year," and it technically is, although 2013 just began days ago. For now, we decide we cannot do nothing, and try Interferon. Gavin's room at the clinic is an infusion room, which is new to us. Usually he is in an exam room for lab draws and check-ups. He is wearing his favorite John Cena shirt that loudly states, "Never Give Up." We felt it was perfect for the day.

Gavin sits on the bed, with a mask on, staring forward. "Buddy, it's going to be a poke in your leg," I tell him.

"Will it be fast?" he asks, turning to the nurse.

"I will count and do it as fast as I can," she assures.

I'm hoping he doesn't have a reaction, and wish I knew it would even work. It hurts to see him so quiet and meek. He is usually witty and chatty. We cheer him on, telling him how brave he is.

"One, two, three." The nurse counts as she injects the medicine on three.

"It stings! It stings! Ouch!" he cries.

I hold his hand, waiting for the pain to stop. He is squeezing so tight. I know it hurts. Steve tells him it's over, and now we wait. The nurse watches the injection site for the first few minutes as well as his oxygen and heart rate. He appears to be handling it fine. He watches the TV but doesn't seem to engage much. The hour passes slowly and quietly and then we are on our way to Neurosurgery.

As we drive over the Mississippi River to St. Paul, anxiety begins to rear its ugly head. I feel dizzy and lightheaded as we go over the new 35W bridge. I worry about what we will discuss, and what Gavin's neurosurgeon feels we can do at this point. As we get off the elevator and take a left into the neurosurgery clinic, I wish it wasn't so. My steps are heavy as we check in at the front desk.

We wait in the room we have been in many times before, the green walls bright and cheery. If these walls could talk, I think. I wonder what they would say? I wonder how many worried parents awaited news that would change their lives forever. I wonder if today will be no different for us.

When the door opens, Dr. Petronio is with a young woman who I have not met before. He explains she is going to take Gavin, and play with him while we talk. My stomach is in knots. He has never had Gavin leave the room. This is it, I fear.

"Mom and Dad, I don't want to go," Gavin begs.

"What's your favorite cartoon?" the polite young woman asks.

He begins to tell her about his favorites, as they walk out the door. "See you soon Gav," I say as the door shuts behind them.

We look at the scans with Dr. Petronio. He tells us the growth is significant, and it appears most of his work has been erased. At the recent brain tumor meeting, some of his colleagues have asked him when is enough, enough. As I listen, I feel like I am having an out-of-body experience. How can doctors be giving up on him? How dare they question this boy who is not giving up! As he continues, Steve and I listen quietly. We usually have more questions, and more hope in our conversations with him. I know if I open my mouth or make eye contact, I will be sobbing. I look at Dr. Petronio, wishing he was not talking about my child.

"I believe I can get more tumor out, but it has gotten to a point, where I don't think I can fully remove it," he continues. My worst fear is happening and the tears are filling my eyes and falling to the floor. Steve, who is always my rock, is full of pain and cannot speak either.

Dr. Petronio continues, knowing we need to hear it all. "We cannot keep putting him through craniotomies, because the risk will begin to outweigh any benefits," He pauses, waiting for one of us to interject.

"You are quiet," he says with concern.

With a deep breath, and a long pause, I manage to form words, "What if we don't do the surgery, then what?"

"If I do not do the surgery, Gavin will slowly lose motor function. His body will deteriorate, losing basic functions, and he would pass away within a few months. I think I can get more tumor though." I feel he is wanting to fight with us too, but has to be sure it is what we want.

"I need to know what you want to do moving forward," he says.

Every ounce of hope seems to have left me at once. Those words, they repeat, and Gavin's death unfolds in my mind. I imagine holding his hand as he takes his last breath and leaves this world. I imagine him losing the ability to walk, talk, eat, and go to the bathroom. I imagine filling his veins with medication until he is a different version of my spirited boy. I vividly picture his lifeless body being peeled from my arms and taken away forever. It all happens in seconds, yet seems in slow motion, too.

Steve doesn't want to cry, and I know that's why he is not saying a word. I could tell him that we are done fighting. Done watching our child, who we love more than anything, suffer. I close my eyes and take a long, steady breath, asking God for some help. How do I make this call? How do I say we are done fighting, when Gavin isn't?

"We are not ready to give up." I manage to say. With a deep breath in and out, I continue.

"Dr. Schultz is working on getting Palbociclib, and we are trying Interferon," I say, trying to convince him, and myself that we have options. I ask him if there is any new technology that could be used on Gavin's tumor. He tells us he will look, and if we want him to operate, he will.

We thank him for meeting with us, knowing it's hard for him too. As we leave the room to get Gavin, Dr. Petronio begins to walk the other direction. Gavin sees him and yells out "Dr. Petronio!" He walks over to him and gives him a big hug. I think it was his way of saying thank you.

Thank you for not giving up on me.

The parking ramp looks and smells different. In fact, everything seems strange and unrecognizable around me. It's like the world changed while we were in there. After buckling Gavin, I put a movie in the DVD player to distract him. I kiss his sweet cheek and get in the front seat. I know if I talk to Steve, we will both end up sobbing. We are not going to do that in front of Gavin so we stay quiet. My soul is destroyed. As we whirl around from the top of the ramp, I am empty.

For a second, I imagine never going back to the hospital and getting out of town. As Steve drives, I stare out the window and replay the words I hoped would never be spoken. I go from hopelessness to anger. I am angry because Gavin has done everything God told him to do. Is this the plan? I demand answers. I have hit a new low I was not sure existed. I look back through the rear view mirror at him and he is smiling and laughing at the movie.

He doesn't know of our conversation. And he won't. Not now. He's six years old and has been through enough. What if more surgery and the Interferon make his life worse? What if he will die anyways and we have just made decisions that will steal the life he has left? Did we make the right decision? When we get home, we get Gavin comfortable and decide to meet in the garage. "I just need to help Dad with something," I tell the kids.

Together, we mourn and hope.

We feel something together we have not experienced before. We have always known this is serious, and Gavin could die. Today though, we had our child's slow and painful death explained, and now it's more real than ever. Gavin is dying.

"I keep hearing it over and over again, it won't stop, babe," I cry. "I can't watch him die! I am the parent, I am supposed to go first, not an innocent child!"

"We won't give up," Steve says while hugging me tight. "Just breathe. We won't give up as long as Gavin wants to fight."

We know how broken we are—how desperate we are to save him. We decide to drive to the local Target to find the movie *Extraordinary Measures*. We had seen it years before, and felt like we were suddenly in a similar situation. Target no longer carries it, so on our way home we stop at Pawn America, a store I had never been to. We walk in and ask if they have the movie. The guy explains that movies are all mixed together, and we would just have to sort through thousands of them.

"I can check the back, but I would start searching over there," the store clerk says as he points to the back half of the store.

We decide to split up and start searching. A minute later, he comes back with the DVD in hand. "That never happens!" he says as he rings it up. He goes on to explain someone must have dropped it off earlier that day. Coincidences have been happening a lot lately. What are the chances of finding the movie? It was like searching for a needle in a haystack.

AT HOME, WE give Gavin meds and start the movie. A father has two children, both with a terminal disease and he finds a medicine that may work. He gets a scientist to agree to work on the medicine, and eventually give it to his children. It worked, curing them of an incurable disease. A parent's determination is strong enough to knock down any barrier. We know we were meant to watch this movie. We are to the end of the rope, but we will never let go. With hope of being able to save our child from dying, we fall asleep.

"I can't breathe!" Gavin yells out.

I look at the clock and it is nearly midnight. Gavin is breathing fast and short breaths. The side effects of Interferon are shortness of breath. "We need to get to a hospital!" I say quickly. After a call to Oncology, we decide to go to the local hospital instead of driving to Children's Hospital. We get there in about ten minutes, even though it's usually about a twenty-minute drive. Little traffic, and maybe a few missed stopped signs, helped.

They don't know Gavin. They try, but it's no comparison to Children's Hospital. They are not sure how to handle Gavin, or me for that matter. I need Gavin to breathe though, and figure they have oxygen. They put a mask on Gavin as he struggles to breathe, and look at him like he's from another planet. The problem list sent over from Children's Hospital is long. We sit with Gavin in the ER while his breaths become steady.

After getting a room at around 4:00 a.m., a nurse comes in to draw labs. She begins to look at Gavin's arm and I stop her. I explain that he has a Hickman line for blood draws.

"What is that?" she asks.

I essentially walk her through the steps. Flush the line, pull back and the blood comes out. It's not that hard, my fatigued brain thinks. By morning, I have slept an hour. I am not pleasant to anyone who comes in because I just don't care. Knowing difficulty breathing is a reaction to the Interferon, I feel we now have one less option from our tiny list of them. Thankfully, we get to go home.

The next few days are dark.

Gavin is better. He is breathing easier without oxygen. But it's deceiving. Craniotomy number five is next week, and we have nothing. Nothing else besides invasive surgery that will cause more deficits. I barely eat or sleep. I pretend to be normal in front of the kids but it's a lie. Steve tries too. He feels the same crippling pain I do.

With nowhere else to go, I turn to prayer. "God, I'm hanging on, but I am afraid I can't any longer. I don't know what to do and I can feel the life in me drain away." On my knees I beg, "Show me, lead me, please." Chemotherapy won't work. Neither will radiation, nor Interferon. If Pfizer can't start a trial, we have failed. Gavin will die.

As Steve and I quietly talk at the dining room table, Grace walks down from her bath, her hair still wet. She has been forgotten in all of this. I still tuck her in, go through the motions, and tell her I love her every day. But I forgot that with the recent scans and talks, she is hurting too.

With tears in her eyes, she stops halfway down the stairs and asks, "Is Gavin going to die?" We have been so careful about what we say around the kids. I wonder if she overheard us?

I want to calm her fears and tell her no, her little brother will not die. Oh, God. How do I answer this? At seven years old, she may have to bury her brother. As I make my way to her, I have no words to comfort her fears, to tell her everything will be okay. I hug her tightly.

"Sweetie, we are going to do everything we can to save Gavin from Joe Bully." I tell her she is such an amazing big sister and I love her. I pray for answers. God, how can I possibly tell her the truth? The truth that we have no way of curing Gavin and are terrified.

I have comforted her through friend problems, and disappointments. Hugged her after she got stitches on her eye lid from a fan. I've sat with her and said whatever happens to us in life, we can only grow from, and learn from. Right now, I am feeling like a giant liar because I don't believe any of it. Right now, I want to tell her how angry I am and how unfair life is. I want to be honest, and tell her that Gavin may die.

I cannot bring myself to those words. Even if it is the truth. For if I speak those words, maybe they will come true. Maybe I will lose Gavin, and life will be meaningless and empty forever. As she gets dressed, and is temporarily distracted from the worry and pain, I walk into Gavin's room and sit on his bed.

"Gavin, I'm so sorry," I whisper as I kiss him goodnight.

Chapter Sixteen

It always seems impossible until it's done.

Nelson Mandela

GAVIN'S LEVEL OF energy has been low the past couple of days. He still laughs and smiles, but it doesn't reach his soul. Since the tumor has grown, I feel a little of him has faded. He is not very hungry these days, eating only a few bites of his favorite foods. He chooses to stay on the couch and not play with his siblings.

As I tuck him in, I ask him if he is okay. What a stupid question, of course he's not okay, *he's dying*. I don't know what to say anymore. How do I do this?

Quickly I add, "Are you scared?"

"No, Mom. Not really. I know God will be with me," he says while staring deep into my eyes.

"I'm just sad that I'm not myself anymore, and I want to be a normal kid again."

I kneel down and say, "I pray for that every day, Gav, and I will never stop."

Nicole Pierson

"Mom, but even though I'm sad about Joe Bully being in my head, I'm really lucky. Some kids don't have a family like I do and that makes me really happy." He is holding my hand. He is comforting me, while going through hell. I embrace his old soul, his way of looking at the big picture of this crazy and unfair world.

"You are right, Gavin. We are all so lucky to have each other. No matter what happens, God is with us and everything will be okay." I allow those words to sink in, convincing myself they are true. I need to believe them. Deep down, I do believe them. I need to remember that as much as I love Gavin, Grace, and Gage, God does too.

I look around his room. His blanket, dinosaurs, baseball hat. I look at all of the things—the Gavin things—surrounding me. I allow myself to truly feel what our life would be without him. As he sleeps, I cry into his pillow and grab his warm hand. The hand that reminds me he is still here. Blood is still running through his veins, and his heart pumps, and his lungs breathe.

In this moment, something washes over me so forcefully, that the crying subsides. All I can hear over and over again in my head, is that I need to push. We have to push for more. I don't know if this was just intuition, or God, but it is undeniable. The realization is, I need to do more. If we give up, so will his medical team. Unless we show determination and hope, nobody else will believe he can survive. Nobody else will fight. It is up to Steve and me to keep hope alive.

If we passively wait for a decision, Pfizer may not start a trial. They have everything to lose. We have a child who might have a chance. Act now, I feel a force inside of me push.

Be Strong and Brave

Things always seem impossible, until they are possible. Gavin always told me that anything is possible to a kid. Over and over again, I rescind my powerful demands of God. To show me His plan when I want to know it. To make things easier, and give me answers. To save my child. After all, I have heard of miracles happening. Children that are cured without explanation, or a tumor that just disappears. Gavin's tumor is relentless and invading. It is destroying the boy he was. How can this be His plan?

Gavin is pushing us though. He is telling us not to give up on him and showing us how to have faith in God's plan. He knows that each surgery has the capacity to drastically change how he thinks, remembers, moves, and lives. Yet, he wants to keep fighting. At six, he has more strength and courage than anyone I have ever met, and I will follow his lead. I will fight as long as he wants to fight.

I decide to set up a Facebook page asking for support. A friend, who has contacts with media, helps me get their attention. Another friend starts an online petition to Pfizer to give the medicine to Gavin. Within twenty-four hours, we have thousands of signatures, and a reporter ready to do a story. In talking with Dr. Schultz, she tells me she will be asking for compassionate use. The trial would take too long to get started, even if approved. We have months, or less.

The compassionate use meeting is tomorrow and they agree to discuss Gavin. Dr. Schultz will be able to talk to the team and make our case. "Is there anything you would like me to add to our conversation?" Dr. Schultz asks.

"Yes. Tell them I won't stop. Tell them I have read every study and I think it is Gavin's only chance to live. If they say no, tell them I will be at their doorstep."

Nicole Pierson

The saying that a parent would go to the ends of the earth for their children is so tangible. It is real.

As I hang up, I am surprised by my boldness. I think of Grace crying that her brother may die. I imagine being with Gavin's things and not Gavin. I imagine a funeral, and am no longer surprised by my behavior. I really will do anything to avoid that level of anguish. The only choice I have is to fight like hell. To tie a knot and hold on tight.

Please Pfizer, fight with us. Be Gavin's miracle.

THE NEXT DAY, I anxiously await a call from Dr. Schultz about the compassionate use meeting. I watch the signatures of the online petition rise to thousands and interact with those who have liked his Facebook page. Putting ourselves out there leads to some interesting comments and views on what we are trying to do. Some people ask me why I would want to try something unproven, and act as if I am irresponsible and selfish for pushing the drug. Some try to give me organic cures to treat my son's cancer. The problem is, he doesn't have cancer. That is a hard thing for people to understand. His tumor is growing uncontrollably and is fatal, but it's not cancer. I reply to all of the suggestions with as much patience as I can. They are just trying to help, I remind myself as each word is typed.

I type out the explanations and tell others about the research I've done. The studies, every single one I had read about the medicine, and about Gavin's tumor. I try and write about the Boswellia medicine, and the many others I was told I should give my child and how they work on cancer cells. Cells that spread to other parts of the body, and act differently than the cells in a growing, mature teratoma. I explain how

Gavin's tumor doesn't spread, it grows in one place. Which in the brain, is just as dangerous as a cancerous tumor that fingers out, in and around the brain. For Gavin, his tumor pushed things out of its way. It bullied its way into space where there was no room. We need to stop the bullying—the growing—so Gavin can have time to heal from the many surgeries. Yet, it won't give us a break. I tell them, and myself, that I would not selfishly give a drug before first determining it is our only hope.

MY PHONE RINGS and it says private number, which means it is Dr. Schultz. I have never wanted to both answer, and not answer, at the same time. "Hello?" I say as I inhale and wait for her tone of voice.

"Hi Nikki, its Kris Ann."

"Hi," I reply quickly, waiting for a response. My palms are sweaty and I feel as if I could faint. Her next words will tell me if our son has a chance at life, or not. The next few seconds, they are everything.

"They are considering," she continues. My tense shoulders relax, and a wave of hope washes over me as I continue to listen. She explains they will see if he's a candidate by testing a tumor tissue sample. For further consideration, it will have to contain a certain protein, called Retinoblastoma. The medicine targets this protein that is causing the growth. The plan is to send a specimen from surgery Monday, and they will test it.

Dr. Schultz tells me the processes for testing, compassionate use approval, investigator site approval, and FDA approval. It seems like a lot. Yet, it seems possible. "Thank you so much Dr. Schultz!" I say with such deep appreciation for her. As bad as things are, she is willing to fight for Gavin and jump through all of the hoops. We are not certain everything will work out, and Gavin will get the drug, nor are we guaranteed that the drug will work. Yet, I feel peace. In a few short moments, I went from empty to hope. I can look at Gavin, and tell him we are working on something. As I prepare him for another brain surgery, we don't feel it is for nothing because we might have a chance.

TOMORROW WE GO in for a fifth craniotomy. More of his skull will be opened, and his brain exposed. As carefully as possible, Dr. Petronio will remove as much tumor as possible, to give Gavin's brain the space it needs to function. I am wide awake, staring into darkness as the rest of my family sleeps. The comments from strangers fill my head. Am I making the right decision? Can Gavin handle another surgery? I ask questions and have no answers. Blindly, in the vast darkness, we are taking each step with faith.

I realize how selfish it may appear to be putting Gavin through another surgery that will not cure, and only prolong life. I know his chances are slim, even if the surgery goes well, and even if we get the medicine. We need a lot of things to happen, and they seem very far from our reach. But, I will never stop reaching because Gavin believes he will make it.

Grace and Gage are sleeping at Grandma and Grandpa's. They are coming to surgery in the morning. I will get some quality time with them finally, for about twenty hours. Because that is how long these surgeries take. I am sad that my quality time with them, means their brother will be in brain surgery. I begin to think about all they have missed since this began. I miss being happy for them, and being a family.

They deserve so much more. After my mind cannot possibly think through things any further, I try to sleep. All night, I have nightmares about all of the things that can happen in brain surgery. I wake up at 4:00 a.m., and decide to have coffee. Like it's a normal day. Which I guess for us, it is.

I wake Gavin so that I can give him some Ativan, an anti-anxiety medication. I know he will be anxious on the way to the hospital as he has been so many times before. He asks where his sister and brother are, and I remind him they are meeting us there. He takes the Ativan and falls asleep on the couch while Steve and I gather our hospital bags. By now, we know what we need while there, and can assume it will be at least a week-long stay.

As we check in, the woman at registration gives us a look of sympathy, knowing how many times we have checked in before. She knows that although we are the first there at 6:00 a.m., Gavin's surgery will last the longest. Like zombies, we walk to pre-op. Gavin is still sleepy, thanks to the anxiety medicine. After getting him in the bed, I give the nurse a list of Gavin's medications and the last time he took them. Thankfully, he is hooked up easily with his Hickman line that comes out of his chest. As the nurse flushes his line with saline, I try to ignore the scars. The large one near his ribs, from being prone during a twenty-hour surgery. The scars from his G-tube, shunt exit site, and port. His head, a battlefield, soon to be cut again.

As they wheel Gavin to the OR, I feel like I am watching from afar and the past seven months isn't really our life. The tumor is already causing so many problems, and growth of any amount could cause a domino effect of life-

Nicole Pierson

threatening issues. We sign the paperwork and watch Gavin's body become lifeless from anesthesia.

WAITING WHILE GAVIN is in brain surgery is a double-edged sword. I wish I could sleep when he sleeps, so I wouldn't have to worry. Yet, I don't want to miss anything. Good or bad, I need to hear the updates.

I hug Gage while he sits on my lap. I kiss his cheek and tell him how much I love him. He is just three, and I have not been able to do things I did with his siblings at his age. I promise him we will do fun things again, but wonder how I could ever have fun again if I lose Gavin. Grace is smiling and coloring pictures for all of us. She tries to brighten the mood and I am in awe of her strength. I sit quietly, and wait for update after update. They come in hourly, just as they have in surgeries before. Dr. Schultz is in the OR today, to see Joe Bully up close. Dr. Petronio is using a new tool today that may help soften the tumor and allow for more tissue to be removed.

After a couple hours, Dr. Schultz comes out to the waiting room, explaining that Dr. Petronio is working diligently and she will update us as soon as she hears anything from Pfizer. She is hopeful with us, and after she leaves, our spirits are lifted. We get through the rest of the day with food, crossword puzzles, and conversation.

At midnight, most have gone home and Steve and I sit holding hands. By the time we get to the PICU, we are both so tired. We made our bed next to Gavin and crashed. He is stable and will not be off sedation until morning. The nurses were still getting all of the lines and tubes situated as my eyes close. The sound of the ventilator is oddly soothing. I ignore the reason we need it, and pretend it's something else. Sometimes, so I don't break, I have to alter my reality. This was one of those moments.

IT IS CLEAR this surgery was hard on Gavin. By morning, he is waking up, but only for a few moments before falling asleep again. When he does open his eyes, they are so far up and to the right, we mostly see white. It takes so much effort each time he tries. Usually, he is awake and alert by now, pointing to the tube because he wants it out. The nurses are watching Gavin every minute, waiting for the right time to remove his ventilator.

We cannot make his brain heal faster. We cannot change what has been done in the process of getting to Joe Bully. Dr. Petronio stops by and tells us the surgery went well, but was more invasive, which is why Gavin may take longer to wake up. He thinks he removed about 30-40% of the tumor, which should give Gavin's brain more room to function.

Every time Gavin moves, I walk over to him, thinking he is going to start waking up. Even with the ventilator now out, he sleeps all day. At first, we thought maybe the sedation drugs were the culprit. We even change his pain medication, thinking he was too comfortable to wake up, but it makes no difference.

The intensivist is a little concerned he is not able to wake up often, and is very sleepy. However, he witnessed Gavin waving to the nurse practitioner Julie, telling us he wanted sausage for breakfast, and squeezing his hand on command. He is neurologically there at times, but not all that often. These moments last a few seconds and he's out again.

Nicole Pierson

Since removing the ventilator, Gavin has had trouble coughing in a productive manner too, so the respiratory specialists are monitoring him closely.

They brought in a vest that helps massage his chest and break up all of the crud in his lungs. He gets to wear it for a few minutes every two hours for now. It is loud, yet it barely arouses him. He has been signing a lot rather than talking, and it seems like waking up enough to open his eyes and have a conversation, is a daunting task. When he does give us a few words, they are timid and quiet, still raspy from the ventilator.

Outside, the snow falls while we wait. Like the past three days of Gavin's recovery, it comes down slowly, just enough to make the ground white.

I think back to the moment we sat in Dr. Petronio's office, hearing exactly how Gavin's life would end. When Dr. Petronio said he would lose motor function, deteriorate, and pass away if we did nothing. I could not do it. I could not give up. Yet, as I now watch Gavin struggle to do anything, I wonder if we made the right decision. It's an awful mind game I cannot seem to stop playing. The thing is, I don't have all of the answers. I just know our decision to go ahead with the surgery was based on Gavin's will to keep fighting. It was Gavin's faith, that got us here.

We are waiting for results of the tumor sample, to determine if Gavin will be given compassionate use. Dr. Petronio is looking for new technology. We are all in, ready to continue this fight. Nobody is giving up, but we are missing something.

The Gavin we had, seems to be gone.

Be Strong and Brave

Chapter Seventeen

There are two ways to live your life.
One is as though nothing is a miracle,
the other is as though everything is a miracle.

Albert Einstein.

GAVIN HAS ALWAYS led us. He has always bravely shown us his tolerance, and ability to recover from surgery. He came back to us after slipping into a coma, and survived a quarter sized blood clot in his brain. Up to this point, he always exceeded expectations, and we were simply in the boat paddling behind him. Now though, he is too weak. He cannot show us the way. He always carried us, and now it's our turn to carry him.

As we watch Gavin struggle to wake up, we are now days out of surgery. Usually by now, there is talk of going home. This time however, there is talk of going to Gillette Children's Hospital, which is a rehabilitation hospital. It is also in St. Paul, just a few minutes away. There, Gavin would be able to get more intense therapy that would hopefully help his brain wake up. Tomorrow, we will talk with the team and decide if this is what we will do.

"Mom, I am hungry," Gavin whispers softly.

"Okay, Gav, what should I order you?" I reply, but he's already sleeping again.

A few minutes later, he mutters, "Mac n' cheese," before he is out again. His eyes never opened during both of these short moments of wakefulness. I go over to the phone and dial nutrition.

"Hi, I would like to place an order for Gavin, in PICU room four," I say as cheerfully as I can manage. "Okay, go ahead," the pleasant young woman says on the other end. "Could I please get macaroni and cheese and some milk?" As I order, like I have many times before, I stare out the window at the frozen city. I see the Xcel Energy center, and the science museum. The smoke is forcefully coming out of the buildings downtown.

I do not listen to the rest of the conversation, yet must have responded in some manner. As I put the phone down, I remember how much Gavin loved the science museum. He always knew more than the exhibit leaders, and remembered every single thing he learned. He loved to run up and down the musical stairs, and would race his sister to the top every time. The trip usually ended with getting ice cream or something at the gift shop. Gavin loved to learn, explore, and play.

It is such a different life than he has now. I can't even imagine Gavin doing what he once could. Oh my, what have we done? If this is his life now, what if it never gets better? I will never forgive myself for signing those papers before surgery. I am crying now, as I imagine his life never getting back to what it was. We are so far away from what we had, how could we possibly get it back?

I HEAR FOOTSTEPS outside our door, and quickly wipe my tears. I go over to Gavin's bed and sit next to Steve, who is holding Gavin's hand, and watching NCIS. The floor doctor says he has great news. Because Gavin has been breathing on his own, and his vitals are good, we are moving to the medical/surgery floor. I am glad for this news, so Gavin can have more visitors, but hoped by this time he would be walking there. Instead, he is sleeping, unaware of any of this.

The smell of the cheese and noodles is enough to get Gavin's eyes to slightly open. He flutters them, trying hard to keep them open. "Buddy, you need to wake up to eat this yummy mac n' cheese!" I say with excitement in my voice. He signs back to me "Eat, now." I give him a bite and he chews a few times. He falls asleep with the food still in his mouth, so I wake him and ask him to swallow his food.

By the third bite, he is a little more alert and manages to say "Mmmmm, cheesy heaven." He makes us laugh— something we haven't done for awhile. He cannot stay awake for more than a few minutes, yet he is his witty self. This brings some comfort. My sweet boy, I wish I could make this easier for you. Thanks for showing us, you are still here.

It is like he has narcolepsy. I email with his neuropsychologist about it. She says it seems like a Reticular Activating System issue (RAS). I guess this system is important. It regulates the shift between sleep and wakefulness. I asked her if this is damaged, then what? She unfortunately doesn't know. She said it's just not every day that someone's RAS has been damaged.

The brain is very plastic. Meaning, it can change and when injured, can create new pathways to perform functions. Gavin's amazing recovery with pure word deafness proves how his brain has the capacity to heal and change. However, this is a different issue and may not recover. He may have permanent damage to his brain.

We never meant for this. Gavin how he is now, is not what we were fighting for. He may be like this forever. Even if we get the medicine, maybe we are too late. I was never fighting for this life. I was fighting for Gavin to be able to find joy again, like a six-year-old should. This, is not what any of us wanted. I feel sick as my memories of what was, and the reality of what is, crash together. I imagine a future of being bed-ridden or in a wheelchair that he cannot even operate himself. I imagine his siblings never being able to play with him in the same way. I imagine having to let go of our dreams that he might graduate high school some day or get married.

"Gavin, please come back to us," I say, as I hold his hand. I sob quietly as I allow myself to let go of dreams of a life he once had. A painful release. During many months of fighting, I could see us going back to our old life. Now, that life is gone.

While he recovers, we continue our online campaign asking people to fight with us. We decide to involve the media and do an interview with TV station, Kare11's Lindsey Seavert. She gives us time to tell our community how desperate we are for a cure, and how Pfizer may have it. As I watch the story on the ten o'clock news, it's odd seeing myself on TV. The story is done well, and I pray it helps us get the medicine he so desperately needs.

GRACE'S HAIR IS wet from her bath, as I brush out the snarls. I long for Gavin to be home with us. Steve is with Gavin and we just did FaceTime to say goodnight. He waved at us, and quietly said good night. Steve and Gavin will be going to Gillette Children's Hospital within the next few days. The plan is the kids and I will go visit most days after school. It is going to be a tough week going back.

Gage cheerfully hugs me before laying down. I am kneeling at his bedside to tuck him in. "Mom, Gavin will be home soon okay?" Gage, at three, knows when I am sad. He can sense that I wish Gavin and Steve were with us. Grace ends up coming to my room because she can't fall asleep. A few minutes later, Gage is with us too. All snuggled in my bed, they fall asleep. I am tempted to climb out of bed like I have so many nights before, to read more. I know I have already read it all, more than once. So I just lie here, in the silence, and listen to the beats of Gage's heart. I text Steve one more time to say I love them and will call in the morning.

Thankfully, my good friend Shannon, who is also Gavin's godparent, is a daycare provider minutes from my house. I drop the kids off before work and know they are safe and will be well cared for. As I drive to work, I listen to the talk show I have listened to many mornings before, but it sounds different. As I press the gas when the light turns green, I do so without the effort I had before. I don't want to keep moving in this life, while leaving Gavin behind.

Nicole Pierson

A song plays on the radio, bringing me to tears with no warning. I imagine Gavin in the condition he is in, and I know that based on the results we will get soon, his days may be numbered. If all options have been tried, I fear we will have to let go. I am hopeful though, and I am trying to have faith like Gavin.

As I pull in to the parking lot at work, I pull myself together. I decide that I will keep answers general to avoid crying. If people ask, I will say Gavin is still recovering. I quickly head to my room to plan for the day. Evaluating equations, I can handle that. As the students come in, I go through the motions and teach them how to substitute for a variable. As I am talking, my mind is elsewhere. Luckily I have taught this content for nearly ten years, so I hope the students don't notice. I give them time to start homework, but really, I just need the time to sit down and compose myself.

After three class periods of going through the motions, I await an update from Steve. I choose not to eat with other teachers, and sit in my room for lunch. I text Steve asking him to call, and he texts back that he is talking to the doctor and will call in a few minutes. I sit very still and stare at nothing in particular. I wait for what seems like a half hour. In reality it is about seven minutes.

"Hello!" I answer quickly, and wait for any news.

"Are you sitting down?" Steve asks.

"Yes, what doctor were you talking to? What's wrong?" I immediately go there.

"Dr. Bendel said that the test results showed Gavin's tumor tested positive for the Retinoblastoma protein!" He tells me we have a chance.

My mind is racing as I think about what this means and quickly reply, "Does this mean they will they give him the medicine?"

"It means that Pfizer has what they need to make a final decision," he explains. I am now crying, knowing we have a real chance for getting the medicine. I am crying because my child might not die. These are the happiest tears I have ever had in my life.

THIS GLIMPSE OF hope was enough to help me finish work, pick up the kids, and make it to the hospital by five. The kids climb up to Gavin's bed and sit on each side. Grace adjusts his pillow and says "Here bud, your neck looks uncomfortable."

We sat with Gavin, watched a movie, and ate dinner together. Before leaving I sit on Gavin's bed and stroke his cheek. He can barely keep his eyes open.

"Gavin, the doctors are trying to get Joe Bully medicine for you. You just have to keep fighting, every day," I say softly.

"I know, Mom," he says, knowing what an uphill climb it is going to be. "I will never give up," he says as his eyes close.

"You are Mommy's little miracle," I say as I kiss his forehead and head home.

Miracles are in the eye of the beholder. I think sometimes the word is used to describe everyday things. Maybe someone hits all the green lights on the way to work and calls it a miracle, or gets something they have prayed for. I never really believed in miracles in the way most people do. I never thought things would just happen because I wanted them to, which is why months ago, I began searching for a cure. I never thought one would just be found and delivered on a silver platter. It sure would have been nice, though.

Webster defines a miracle as "an effect or extraordinary event in the physical world that surpasses all known human or natural powers and is ascribed to a supernatural cause." Using that definition, it seems like hard work doesn't matter, and that miracles are only explained by something beyond what is known.

When God came to Gavin, and told him to be strong and brave, we didn't know the tumor would grow. We had no clue how many surgeries he would endure, or what complications would arise. It was during those times we followed Gavin's faith. He showed Himself to Gavin, so Gavin would be able to face the challenges, the pain, and suffering. God is here each day, telling us to be courageous and not to be afraid.

So we wait, for our miracle, even if it takes time.

THE NEXT MORNING while at work, Steve gives me a morning update. During my prep, I call to see how physical therapy went. Gavin managed to take a few steps with much assistance, which is progress. He is still very tired though, and sometimes falls asleep during his sessions.

About ten minutes after I hang up, he calls back. "Is everything okay?" I say, bypassing a greeting.

"Yes, it is. In fact, it is more than okay," he replies.

"What do you mean, what's going on?" I say impatiently.

"I just went to get lunch and ran into Dr. Petronio on the elevator. I asked him if he heard the good news about possibly getting the medicine and he replied by saying he had good news too," Steve says all in one breath.

"Okay, what is it?" I reply impatiently.

"He said he found a laser, one that is minimally invasive and could reach hard-to-get areas of the tumor. I asked him about the parts that grew recently that he didn't think he would ever be able to remove, and he said he thinks this tool could reach those too!" Steve explains the entire conversation knowing I will ask more questions if he doesn't.

"Oh my God!" I say, in shock about what this could mean.

Two weeks ago, we sat in Dr. Petronio's office—hearing that without something, Gavin will die. I asked if there was any new technology we could use. I told Dr. Petronio that I would work on getting the medicine, and he said he would look into new techniques that may be able to get to the tumor. Since then, he has found something! Something that may save Gavin's life. Dr. Petronio will be talking to the hospital board about getting the tool and using it on Gavin.

A miracle just happened in the elevator at Children's Hospital. Just a few days ago, Gavin had a zero percent chance of survival. Now, two treatments have come up. I cannot help but think God has led us to this. He did not drop a miracle on our doorstep, but Gavin followed his command. He was strong and brave, and he led us with his unwavering faith.

The next day, Pfizer notifies Gavin's team they have approved Gavin for compassionate use, and are working on getting it to us.

Your miracles are coming Gavin, just hold on.

Nicole Pierson

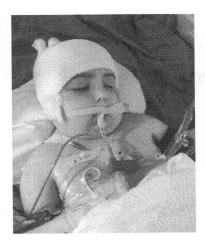

Gavin after fifth craniotomy in January 2013. Waiting for a cure.

Gavin and Gage during one of our visits, a moment Gavin happened to be awake for a few minutes.

Be Strong and Brave

Chapter Eighteen

Fear not, for I am with you, be not dismayed,
    for I am your God:
I will strengthen you, I will help you.
I will uphold you with my victorious right hand.

Isaiah 41:10.

BY THE END of the week, Gavin has not made much progress
and is moved to Gillette Children's Hospital for rehab. I get
there as quickly as possible after picking up the kids. It's
Friday, and Steve is going to go home for the weekend while
I stay with Gavin. As I walk to Gavin's room, I notice that the
children here are facing many struggles. Some are unable to
walk, talk, and move independently. It dawns on me that
Gavin is walking these same halls and also has many things he
cannot do. Of course I knew that, which is why we wanted
him here. Yet, it feels as if I have just hit a wall. A very high,
unbreakable wall of realizing that this could be Gavin's life
forever.

Nicole Pierson

I look at him and see a wheelchair rather than the child I know. I see equipment which helps him do everyday tasks. This is both terrifying and harrowing. I know my son is in this unable body, but I can't see him. His head is tilted to the right, eyes only able to be fixated up and to the right. His arms and legs are weak, being held in place with straps. His cheeks puffy from steroids, and his soul... Where is his soul?

After Steve and the kids leave for the night, the nurse comes in to tell me she wants to give him a bath. Two nurses move Gavin from his bed to a standing wheelchair. I have never experienced this before, so I just watch and follow. He is wheeled across the hall to the bathing room, which consists of a giant tub allowing children in wheelchairs to be submersed. I am not in my comfort zone. I watch as Gavin is lowered into the bathtub. He is awake but just staring beyond me, incapable of taking care of himself, moving himself, or bathing himself. This is where we are. This is what five invasive craniotomies look like.

I help the nurse wash Gavin and he quietly tells me the water feels nice, although it takes much effort to do so. He falls asleep before it's over, and the nurse dresses him back in his room. I am traumatized by this experience because I cannot help but wonder if he will get better. I don't know how he will come back from this. We may get the medicine, and we may even have a laser, but if this is his quality of life, God, this is not what we wanted.

Throughout the weekend, I chat with other moms who have children who are permanently disabled in the way Gavin is right now. I see their world and how their other children's lives are affected by the twenty-four hour care their child needs. I bring Gavin to various therapy sessions where his physical therapy consists of holding his head up and rolling over. I try to be encouraging, but feel just as paralyzed as Gavin.

Excited that Gavin gets a day pass, we go to the Mall of America's Sea Life. Gavin loves this place and has been here many times before. He used to run around inside the underwater aquarium, where sea turtles and sharks swam around. He would point out all of the different species and climb up the wall onto the ledge to get a closer look. Today, as we wheel him around in his wheelchair, he sleeps. The water and sea creatures whirl above and around us while I adjust Gavin's head when it falls too much to the side. Once in a while he wakes up, flutters his eyes before falling asleep again quickly.

We bring him back to the hospital, defeated.

The next day at Gillette Children's Hospital, we decide the extra therapy has not been effective. He can't even stay awake long enough to do therapy. Also, he looks very pale, so Children's Hospital has a few tests they would like to run. He will soon be moved back to continue recovering there. Grace, Gage and I have begun our week of school and hospital, as we did all of last week. When we get to Gavin's hallway, Grace and Gage run ahead, so excited to see their brother. As we enter the room, they quiet down as they realize Gavin is sleeping. I am not surprised to see him sleeping, as it's what he does most of the day.

Grace holds Gavin's hand and can see past the reality. She knows, somewhere underneath the steroid cheeks and tired body, is her brother. She stares at him, waiting for him to wake up. Steve and I discuss logistics about moving back to Children's Hospital as the kids sit in bed with Gavin.

Nicole Pierson

SpongeBob plays on the TV, and once in a while Gavin repeats a word or two. Steve and I sit in absolute exhaustion.

"Tomorrow I am going to stop at the Minneapolis pharmacy before coming over to St. Paul," I say softly as to not interrupt the cartoon. I will be picking up the medicine that may save his life, but first, we need Gavin to come back to us. We need his fighting spirit to continue to lead us.

Before we leave, Grace closes her eyes and puts her head gently on Gavin's chest. "Dear God, please watch over my brother because he is my best friend. I hope your plan is to let Gavin stay on earth for a long time. I hope that he will be our little miracle. Amen."

I am holding back tears as I realize how grown up she sounds. My heart feels heavy because I pray for the same things. Grace misses her best friend, her partner in crime, even if he did tell on her when she was naughty. Like the time they were toddlers and I found them in the washer, bubbles filling up around them. I turned the corner to the laundry room and they were standing in the washer, splashing about. Gavin's eye caught mine first and he nudged his big sister to turn around. Within seconds, Gavin told me that Grace put the soap in and pressed the buttons. He was always too honest, and she always got mad at him for telling.

Then he would chase her around the house apologizing. "Grace, I am so sorry please forgive me." He hated if someone was angry with him and would do anything to get his best friend back. They did everything together, and even compromised on playing with their favorite toys. Gavin would take out his dinosaurs and they would be Barbie's pets. The playhouse doubled as a princess castle and a knight's warzone.

Now, the playhouse sits empty. Toys still in it from last summer, when Gavin spent his days in the hospital. I remember the last day they played in it together, just two days before Gavin's diagnosis. I took a picture of them peering through the wooden spindles of the front porch. They were so happy and free in that picture. God, please let them be again.

I lean over and kiss Gavin's forehead. As we walk out, my steps are unwilling. Grace and Gage are forcing me forward as they run ahead. I can't help but feel as if I am leaving Gavin behind, chasing my two healthy children. I buckle up and begin driving down the twirling exit of the ramp. The kids squeal as we go round and round. A moment of joy, followed by a drive home of sorrow.

We have a DVD player in our vehicle. This has been handy on many occasions. Like the long trip we took to Wisconsin Dells a few weeks before Gavin began this journey. What was supposed to be a few hours, turned out to be nearly five, due to a semi-truck on fire on Highway 94. The kids watched movies as we sat still on the highway for over an hour. I was so thankful for the DVD player. Tonight, I press play so I can cry without the kids noticing.

Gavin is so far from the child he was. Even with a new stimulant medication added, Gavin cannot stay awake for more than about thirty minutes. When he is awake, he stares upward and barely speaks. His voice, when he manages to say a few words, is raspy and tired. He is completely dependent on care twenty-four hours a day. My eyes eventually dry out and I tell myself we can only go forward. This has to be the bottom. This has to be hell.

Nicole Pierson

It is the worst place we have ever been, and we have to climb out of this hole. I fall to my bed, worn out from my drive home and a long day. How can this be happening? After all these months of fighting, I feel depleted. I cuddle with Grace and Gage but am distant. Part of me is back at the hospital with Gavin, trying to tell him to keep fighting. Come on, Gavin, keep going.

I DROP THE kids off and head to the pharmacy. I am nervous as I park and walk towards the pharmacy. When a patient receives a trial drug, they have to pick it up at the investigator site, which is Minneapolis Children's. I have been here so many times, and it seems odd that I will just pick this medicine up like any other. We worked so hard to get it that I thought I would have to jump a few more hoops or give my right hand in exchange.

"I am here to pick up Palbociclib for Gavin Pierson," I say to the woman at the counter.

She asks for his date of birth and address as she looks it up on the computer. So far, nobody has requested a limb. "Okay I'll be right back," she says, without asking any special questions. So far, this seems too easy.

She brings back what looks like any other plastic bottle. It's a white, rectangular shaped plastic bottle with Gavin's name on it. She explains he must not eat an hour before or after taking the two oral capsules in the morning. She doesn't have much more than that, and even what she told me came right from the directions on the label. I suspect that I know more about the drug than she does, so when she asks if I have any questions, I simply say no.

I sign my name and walk away.

After months of asking for this medicine, I am holding this bottle. We actually did it. I don't know how we did, but the evidence is in my hands. I handle the bottle like it's a new baby and head to St. Paul.

I am somewhat relieved when I walk into the St. Paul Children's Hospital campus. We spent our summer here, and much of the fall. It is our second home and everyone knows Gavin. He is in the neurology unit because they are going to do an EEG overnight. They want to be sure he is not having seizures with his staring episodes. He is quiet as they glue all of the electrodes on his head.

I give Steve the medicine as he will be guarding it overnight. Tomorrow, Gavin will take the pills in the morning and they have to draw labs at very specific intervals to check the levels of medication in his blood. Being the first pediatric patient, they have to determine the correct dosing. At this point, they started with half the adult dose.

"Look Gavin, here is the Joe Bully medicine," I say as I hold up the bottle in his line of sight. His eyes still cannot move down well and tend to stay to the right. He half smiles but that's all he can manage. I head home with something I had been lacking. Hope. I have to think of better days ahead. This medicine has to work. Gavin has to get better.

The first dose of the medicine is given at 9:30 a.m. on February 6. It is a fairly quiet day with the scheduled labs and results from the EEG. The neurologist tells Steve that the EEG showed no seizures, but slow brain waves. I am not surprised, as I feel like Gavin is in slow motion. Like his brain is needing a time out. Labs also show Gavin's hemoglobin is low enough to warrant a blood transfusion. By the end of the day, he also tested positive for C-diff, a bacterial infection.

Nicole Pierson

All of this today has rained on our parade. He was starting the medicine today, we were excited and trying to be forward in our thinking. Things were supposed to start improving. We know better though. Murphy's Law gets us every time. Anything that can go wrong, will go wrong. We hope that a blood transfusion, abnormal EEG, and C-diff is all for today though.

IN THE SILENCE and darkness, Gavin screams nonsense. It wakes me up and I run to his side. He is sleep talking, except none of it makes any sense. It is a side effect of the stimulant medication. I feel like I am getting some insight to his disorganized brain when this happens. I imagine all kinds of neurons firing trying to reconnect. We are home now, and Gavin hasn't changed much. We started a stimulant medication hoping to help him wake up, but all it is doing is confusing him. My hope is that being home, around his siblings and family, he will return to us. I miss having conversations with him. I miss his jokes, and his strength.

He will talk, but it's quiet and timid. He does not initiate any conversation, just sits there. Yesterday, our first day home, I went over to check on him on the couch, thinking he was watching cartoons. He was staring at the wall. I turned him a little so he could see the TV but he didn't seem to care either way. He is just not here.

I sing familiar songs to him and even when he doesn't say much, I talk about things he likes. I read him dinosaur books and talk about things we could do in the future. I am trying to show him the life he had, so that maybe he will want it back. We are upbeat and happy around him, hoping this will motivate him to be the same. Our goal today is to get him up four times to walk. "Buddy, Mom and Dad are going to help you walk, okay?" I say to him before moving him.

It takes a lot of effort to sit him up, so we get there and wait a few minutes. He doesn't say anything. Steve holds his waist while I put my hands under his arms to lift him to a standing position. Our goal is about ten feet and back. Each step he attempts is shaky and unsteady, even with support. It is like helping a baby learn to walk, except he's six. I try not to pour myself too much into those thoughts and continue to encourage him to take another step. He leans on me a lot and his knees give out on him before we make it back to the couch. Steve lifts him onto the couch and we're done. That's one time. Three more to go.

FOR NOW, GAVIN will use a wheelchair to go long distances. At least I tell myself it's for now. He has been taking Palbocilcib, the drug from Pfizer, for two weeks. He has not magically regained his balance, or overcome his extreme fatigue. The drug is in pill form, which was tricky at first but he now has it figured out. With each pill he swallows, I imagine more of him coming back to me.

Being nearly a month out from surgery, not much has changed. Gavin's eyes are still very much up and to the right most of the time. He can move them towards the middle but it takes great effort. Today we are taking Gavin to the Mayo Clinic to see a neuro-ophthalmologist. Hopefully we can get some answers about his eyes and learn if he's a candidate for surgery.

As we wait in the waiting area, I see the stares. I see how they stare at him, yet past him at the same time. Like he's not Gavin, like he is just a body in a wheelchair. I get it, that is what it looks like. But I still imagine him climbing and running and flipping. "Gavin Pierson," a nurse says as she walks out to the waiting area. "That's us," I reply while wheeling Gavin over to her.

The doctor tells us nothing we don't already know.

"I could do surgery to move his eyes over, but it wouldn't help them work any better," he begins.

He explains that Gavin's eyes and brain need to work together, and right now they are not doing that well. By the end of the appointment, we learn that Gavin has a right field cut, gaze paresis, and oculomotor deficiency. These may or may not improve with time. Although I am concerned about his eyes, I cannot even go there right now. I feel that getting him to chat more, be present, learn to walk again need our prime attention.

What are we without the will to live? I feel Gavin has lost this. I ponder this as we drive home from the Mayo Clinic. Gavin has been lost for weeks. His body is here, and sometimes I can feel his soul too, but he just stares at nothing and isn't really here. Things he loves don't pique his interest, and he doesn't joke anymore. I fear it is too late to save the boy we had, and that from this point forward we can only hope to save a shadow of who he used to be.

In life, we have to choose our battles. When we think about everything we must do to accomplish something, it is overwhelming. The only way to get to the top of a mountain is to focus on the next move. We cannot look at every part of Gavin's recovery at once, or we will deem it impossible. To get him back, we have to be patient. Our focus now is to help him want to live.

We ask friends and family to visit and bring life into our home. We watch funny movies, sing and dance. We show Gavin a reflection of his old self so he wills himself to try to get it back. Each day he is home, he tries a little more. He engages in the activity and begins to initiate conversation. One day, my Aunt Cathy brought Gavin a microphone toy. She shows him how to yell in it, and he tries, exercising his vocal chords. Steve plays his favorite music, and Gavin will dance with his arms. Although he's not flipping or climbing, he is slowly making purposeful movements and staying awake for longer periods of time.

NEARLY SIX WEEKS after surgery, Gavin says, "Mom, I want to walk!" I immediately go to him, so I can be near him as he tries. Although he nearly falls, and is very shaky with his legs wide apart, he walks from the living room to the kitchen. Afterwards, he says, "Joe Bully, you have to leave this party. I am taking your cake away. Good bye!" As I laugh with him, I hug him so tight. Happy tears that I haven't felt in a while. He is here! My sarcastic little boy is back. I know in this moment, that his will is back.

I watched Gavin make little, if any, progress for over a month. He would put little effort into therapy and had no desire to engage in life. The last couple of days it's like a switch flipped from dim to bright. He suddenly has the strength to fight. As he finishes the first cycle of Palbociclib, he is more himself each day. He jokes more and laughs from his belly. He uses the wheelchair less and walks more. There is even talk of going back to school, although it's a daunting process. He started to get evaluated for school last fall, but then was hospitalized, had a blood clot, and the tumor grew. One thing after another piled up and by the time it was done, he was too dependent to return.

Nearly two months after surgery, Steve begins to bring him for short visits at school. I am nervous for so many reasons. His brain has been through so much and he has been gone from school for a year. Returning is not going to be easy.

"How was it?" I ask during my lunch break. Steve just got home from Gavin's first day at school.

"It was okay, he tried to read a little bit and listened during story time," Steve replies. Gavin gets tired very quickly after just a few tasks.

"I'm sure he just needs time to get used to school again," I reply. Gavin has been in hospitals for the past year, while other kids learned to read, write, and play. They got stronger and taller, while Gavin got weaker. For now, we need to be thankful he can even attend, knowing that besides fighting to live, school will be another mountain to climb. We allow Gavin's brain to heal and take advantage of the moments he has energy.

Our days are filled with ups and downs. We celebrate the smallest of victories, because the big ones are not going to come easily. We celebrate when he remembers something that happened a few minutes ago, or when he recalls a fact he once knew. Slowly, his brain tries to bounce back.

TWO MONTHS' POST-OP, it's time for Gavin's MRI. This is the moment that will tell us if the drug we worked so hard to get, is actually working. In my soul, I know it is. Or at least I make myself believe so. I find myself re-reading all of the studies just to reassure my beliefs.

We drive to St. Paul as we have many times before. Gavin has had dozens of scans, but this one means more. We check in at the welcome desk and head to radiology.

"Hi, Gavin," the nurse says as he sits down by the fish tank.

"Here for another MRI?" The receptionist has the paperwork ready to go.

As I grab it, I reply, "Yes, this is a big one." I walk over and sit with Gavin. To make him laugh I read some of the questions aloud.

"Are you pregnant Gavin?" I begin.

"No! Mom stop!" he laughs.

"Do you have permanent eye liner or tattoos?"

"Mom!" he exclaims.

"Okay, I'll stop. One more though. Are you breast-feeding?"

He shakes his head with a smirk.

"Hi, Gavin, are you ready for your scan?" The radiology nurses know him well, and already have the DVD booklet ready for him to choose a movie. "Yep!" he says cheerfully. I sit at the end of the tube in radiology, holding Gavin's feet. I am so nervous, knowing if it continued to grow on the medicine, we are in bad shape.

"Someone will call with results later today," the tech tells me. Please God, please show us it worked, I pray as we drive home.

I BARELY ALLOW my phone to ring before picking up. On the other end of the line, I am told the MRI shows a stable Joe Bully. The growth has been shut down. Every single emotion I have felt in the past year, is felt at once, with joy and

Nicole Pierson

thankfulness in my heart. We have time! A stable tumor allows us time to think. Time for Gavin to recover. Dr. Petronio is working on getting the laser. We have options for a cure for the first time since the monster grew uncontrollably.

Gavin walks more and more each day. He is regaining energy and not sleeping as much. One weekend, we were granted an overnight trip to the Mall of America thanks to a local foundation that helps children fighting cancer. We had adjoining hotel rooms and the kids' room was filled with toys. The first thing Grace did was jump on the bed. Gage soon followed.

"Come on Gavin!" they squealed.

Hesitant at first, then going all-in, Gavin ran for the bed.

As he jumped, he proclaimed, "I feel like a normal kid again!" Life was breathed into him. After a year of fighting, he is beginning to become the child he used to be.

Chapter Nineteen

Our faith can move mountains.

Matthew 17:20

THE LEAVES ARE beginning to turn into vibrant colors as Gavin and Gage run up the stairs to the playhouse. "Pretend we are running from bad guys and this is our hideout!" Gage calls as he trails behind. "Okay, and I will spy on them through the side window while you guard the door," Gavin replies as he reaches the top.

Play. Laughter. Boys being boys. As I sip coffee on the deck, I find myself in awe of the beauty that surrounds me. I notice the patterns of the branches on the large trees that cross paths overhead. I hear the birds chirping and allow myself to breathe in the crisp fall air.

Other than a minor shunt correction in July, Gavin has spent the summer out of the hospital. He has been getting strength back, and beginning to see words again. His brain, after so much insult, is healing. There are reminders of all he

Nicole Pierson

has endured, but he doesn't let them stop him. His eyes do not move very far up, and cannot move down at all. He has a right field vision cut as well. He still runs and somehow avoids tripping over things or running into things. I really don't know how he does it.

He knows he has a lot of catching up to do in school. He is willing to do the hard work. Our biggest hurdle at the moment, is his mental fatigue after focusing for a while. He hits a wall and is just done, his brain demanding rest. Despite the fatigue, he is looking forward to going back to school and seeing his friends. Riding the bus, playing at recess, and learning. All things he missed for so long.

On the first day of school, Gavin gets on the bus like he did two years ago. He smiles for first-day pictures going off around him. My favorite is Gavin with his two buddies, Crosby and Marshall. He placed one arm around each shoulder with pride. In triumph that he made it to second grade.

IT IS OCTOBER, and we are planning Gavin's first surgery with Visualase laser ablation. Gavin will be the first to use this approach for a mature teratoma. "How are you feeling about surgery, Gav?" Steve asks. "Can we do it tomorrow?" Gavin replies. He wants Joe Bully gone. Knowing he is the first, he is not afraid. He is not discouraged. I cannot imagine being the first to use a new tool, in my brain. It terrifies me. Yet, Gavin has faith it will work, and that someday, Joe Bully will be down forever.

A FILM CREW is going to be following the surgery because of the history that is being made. Today they will use the laser and remove one of the two shunts, as it is no longer needed. Our first update comes about two hours later. Usually the surgery nurse calls my cell. Why are they calling the waiting area desk?

"Mrs. Pierson?" she calls and I am up and on my way to her.

"Gavin is doing fine, but Dr. Petronio would like to talk to you." My heart sinks.

Gavin has been in more than ten brain surgeries with Dr. Petronio, and never has he asked to speak to me during surgery. As I walk quickly to the phone, I am thinking the worst. Dr. Petronio explains to me they had tried to place two laser fibers into Gavin's tumor but the tumor was too difficult to penetrate and they could not get in. The laser fibers were deflected by the bone-like surface of the bully. He asks me what he should do.

"I can close and then all we have done today is remove a shunt. Or I think I can access the tumor from another angle and ablate some of the tumor." I hear something unspoken in Dr. Petronio's voice. I hear the importance of trying again and not giving up yet.

In seconds, I fast forward to the scenario if I choose to say enough is enough. Close and be done. Gavin wakes up to realize the laser that we have been so hopeful would work, did not. Palbociclib would eventually stop working and the tumor would grow. And he would die. Quickly, I tell Dr. Petronio to please try the new angle. I hang up with a deep breath asking God to be with Dr. Petronio. We did not come this far to stop!

I walk over to my family, who are anxiously awaiting to know why Dr. Petronio wanted to talk to me during surgery. They know this has never happened. I explain that he could not get in. I see their faces quickly drain of hope. I explain that I made the call to try again from a different angle. I then sit in silence and wonder what we will do if it doesn't work. I find myself succumbing to fear. I thought I got past that?

The thing about having faith is that even when we consciously do, fear creeps in. Faith is not about being a fair weather fan. It is about believing when it is beyond what we know or think we know.

In this moment, I find my center and wait. I allow fear but also allow hope. It is a balancing act of human emotion and allowing what is, to be. Minutes go by, and I feel as if it has been an hour. I stare at my phone, and triple check that the ringer is on. I then check my missed calls, just in case.

The next update is the biggest exhale we have had in the past year and a half. He got in. Joe Bully was being ablated! In other words, we are finally destroying this monster at its core. The emotion I have the moment I hear these words is overwhelming. I am for the first time feeling as if it will be okay. Gavin will be okay!

I am used to walking in to the PICU expecting ventilators, many nurses, and a sedated child who we hope wakes up resembling the boy we love. As the double doors open, we nod to the familiar faces at the desk and nurses' stations. We walk into the room thinking we know what to expect. But before we can push the curtains aside we stop and listen.

Gavin is talking! In a raspy, soft voice, but he is talking! He just had brain surgery, and he is asking for root beer.

Be Strong and Brave

God, is this what you were waiting for?

In one moment, I felt another shift to our world. I felt the same tingly sensation on my right arm, like someone was touching me and telling me, "see I told you it would be alright." I jolt into the room and kiss Gavin on the cheek. He asks me, "So when are we going to do surgery?"

"It's already done, Buddy," I say. We put a hole right through the bully, I continue to tell him and he cannot believe it. He too, was used to waking up feeling like a different person. At seven, he knew the long road that comes with brain surgery. Therapy, new deficits to accommodate or compensate for, the long list of medications to control basic functions.

None of those are needed.

The next day, we bring Gavin home. The day after that he went trick or treating as a magician.

The recovery mimics the flu. He needs a few days of taking it easy as the tumor reacts to the laser with inflammation. With flushed cheeks and curled up in a blanket, Gavin watches T.V. He needs Tylenol for the first couple of days but is back to school in less than a week. As the tumor shrinks from the ablation, Gavin experiences some dizziness and gets fatigued, but it's nothing like recovery from a craniotomy.

Slowly but surely, Joe Bully is going down. We are on our way to a cure.

JUST WHEN YOU think you have knocked a bully down, they try one last cheap shot. About a month after the laser ablation, I get a concerned call while at work.

"Hello?" I answer quietly at my desk.

"Hi Nicole, this is Ramsey Elementary health office. I just wanted to let you know that Gavin has been complaining of being dizzy," the nurse explains.

"Okay, I can come pick him up, give me about thirty minutes," I say.

When I get there he has his teacher, another teacher, and two nurses around him. He is telling them all about his upcoming trip to Texas in two days. With dad and Brian, a man we met when he volunteered to do a magic party for Gavin, he is attending a comic con event and will get to meet his favorite WWE wrestler, John Cena. He has been counting down to this special trip and excitedly tells them about it.

"Yeah, it's going to be awesome," he continues as I wait. Every few sentences, I hear him slur a word. Other than that, he seems okay. I cancel plans I had with my sister just to monitor him. He seems fine all night and I don't notice anything alarming.

The next day, I send him to school and get no phone calls. Via email, the nurse tells me he seems better. I chalk it up to dehydration or changes as the tumor shrinks from the laser surgery. After school, Gavin packs his bag for a weekend away.

"Hey Gavin, I bet you're tired," I say as I bring his meds over to the couch. "You have a big day tomorrow!"

He doesn't say anything, and I assume it's because he really is tired.

I give him his pill and turn to get his liquid medication. The pill seems to be getting stuck, like he cannot swallow or something. I notice that water had spilled out from Gavin's mouth on one side. His face looks different too, but I can't pinpoint why. Finally, the pill goes down.

Be Strong and Brave

My mind searches the past few days for something that could explain these concerning neurological symptoms. The slurring of speech and dizziness from the day before come to my mind quickly. As he takes the second medication, it happens again.

"Gavin, are you feeling okay?"

"I feeel diiizzzy," he tries.

"Gavin can you smile? Buddy, please try to smile," I plead.

Only one side of his face is moving and a second later I am running up the stairs telling Steve we need to go to the ER. I don't know what, but something is wrong and it's getting worse by the minute. In the car, I sit in back with Gavin as he deteriorates quickly. I call the ER and ask them to page Neurosurgery and tell them that I am very worried. Gavin begins to use sign language after realizing that he cannot form words. He signs to me that his right arm is numb and he cannot feel it.

We barge into the ER as we have many times before, but this time I do not hesitate to let them know this is uncharacteristic, sudden, and he needs a scan.

During the CT scan, Gavin cannot even stand up or hold his head up and ends up vomiting all over. We head back to the room and for some reason I do not know, we are left alone while the scan gets read. Gavin is lethargic yet begins to yell nonsense words. It is frightening and I worry what is happening inside his brain. I page the nurse twice with no response. A couple minutes later, I run out to the nurse station demanding someone come in. I could not believe the number of people just sitting while something so wrong is happening.

Nicole Pierson

One doctor begins to tell me this can be normal with a brain tumor. I do not allow him the courtesy to continue his opinion. "No, this is NOT normal for Gavin!!" I firmly state.

"Well, the scan showed no concerns," he replies.

It's not enough though, they are missing something. If only Dr. Petronio could see Gavin right now, he would be so upset with how nonchalant everyone is being.

After two hours, and more random yelling spells, we are finally admitted upstairs, the place that is comforting because they know Gavin, and Dr. Petronio is only a page away. They administer IV fluids and steroids. Gavin improves slightly.

I know that there is inflammation of some sort, otherwise the steroids wouldn't have made a difference. The next morning a full brain MRI is scheduled to look further at the reason for the stroke-like symptoms last night. We have to tell Gavin he will be missing his flight to Texas.

AS I CUDDLE with Gavin, a team of doctors fill the room. I want to ask them to leave because I know they don't have good news. Their bowed heads and somber aura fills me with anxiety. I look up, holding Gavin's hand, preparing myself for devastation.

"Well, this is very serious." the doctor begins.

"Gavin has an extensive blood clot in his brain. Not like before when it was in one place. All of his veins that drain blood from his brain to his heart are completely clotted," he continues. In shock, I listen with no emotion. I just can't feel it right now. Not in front of all of these doctors, and not in front of Gavin. I listen as he explains Gavin is lucky to be in the state he is, and he needs to say no more. I get it. Gavin is lucky to be alive.

After they leave, the tears fall. I never cry in front of Gavin. I am so scared though. They say it could still get worse and move us to the intensive care unit.

"Mom, please don't cry, I'm going to make it," Gavin says. When I look at him, I see his veins protruding on the side of his head; the veins which are mostly clotted and could end his life. I pray the disaster does not fully develop; that we have caught this early enough to stop it from getting worse.

How does he do it? How does he know my thoughts without me telling him? I hug him tightly and wonder how he is breathing and talking if all of his veins in his brain are clotted. How does that even work?

Collateral veins. That is why he is alive. This must have happened over time and as the large veins clotted, Gavin's body knew to make alternate routes and thus, collateral veins were formed. These minor blood vessels allow some blood flow. However, not enough which is why he began having symptoms.

We begin IV anticoagulants and monitor Gavin for signs of neurological decline. I feel like any minute, a tsunami could happen. Any moment, Gavin could be gone. It's been a long time since we have had an emergency complication like this. It shoves me back into the world of devastation quickly.

As the days go by, and Gavin does not worsen but improve, I wonder what would have happened if I didn't notice the water coming out of the side of his mouth and we didn't bring him in? What if he got on an airplane with all of that pressure in his head?

Nicole Pierson

It is decided that Gavin will be on lovenox—a blood thinner—for a long time. With his history of clots, and the number of neurosurgeries he has had, we are not taking any chances. The veins that were completely clotted will be monitored and should at least partially regain flow.

FOR MONTHS AFTER the scary blood clot, Gavin stays out of the hospital and we go in periodically for scans. The plan is to monitor and use laser ablation as needed. After fighting nonstop, this time is unfamiliar and almost scary. Not calling Oncology or Neurosurgery every other day, we find ways to fill our time.

The medicine Gavin continues to take makes him tired and nauseous at times. Minor things compared to where he has been. I begin to realize I no longer fall asleep afraid he will die. And that once in a while, I allow myself to imagine him growing up. Not knowing if the treatments will cure him is still really tough. I think I have it all together, and one thing can bring me back to the reality that nobody has won this fight before.

At school, his teacher, Mrs. Barrientes, allows him to rest on a beanbag chair when needed. He has a wonderful para, Mrs. Olson, and a special education teacher, Mrs. Aldrich. They push him when they know he can, and know when to let his brain rest. I am trying to figure out how to balance this. I know he is capable and is very intelligent, despite what his brain has endured. Yet, he also needs rest and accommodations. His biggest accomplishment is that he is taking grade level spelling tests and retraining his brain how to read.

Be Strong and Brave

In February 2014, a few months after the first procedure, Gavin has a second ablation surgery. This time, attacking a different part of Joe Bully. Each ablation will be done to target different parts of the tumor until hopefully, someday, Gavin is cured. Again, he is out of the hospital the next day after brain surgery, without neurological deficits. It is night and day when comparing craniotomies to laser ablations. My child wakes up the same child. We are not just playing catch-up, we are slowly killing the bully and once down, he stays there.

The only worry is the laser simply cannot ablate all of the tissue, so our faith is once again all we have. It is enough though, because for now, we have a plan. When Gavin was diagnosed, our life path was changed in one moment. The unknown was terrifying. Yet, as we made a plan to treat him, I felt better again. Because I thought I could predict how our life would go from that point on.

Nope. The tumor grew. Then it grew again and invaded and destroyed. It took my child away a little at a time and we had nothing. No cure, no plan. Again, devastation filled my soul and I yearned to know the future.

Today we have another plan that we hope will become Gavin's cure. However, I am living a different life now—a life of not knowing and being okay with it.

I am learning to let go of what I think life should be, or what I think it will be. Because guess what? All of the planning in the world wouldn't have changed the fact that Gavin had a tumor growing out of control in his brain.

Planning does not equate to knowing.

We cannot know what has yet to happen. So, I don't worry about it. I just do what I have to do today to get through

Nicole Pierson

this thing called life. With Gavin leading me and showing me what faith can do, I am not afraid of the unknown. As we approach his post-op scan, for once, I am not full of fear and anxiety. I am calm, knowing we have done absolutely everything for Gavin. Knowing that God had something big planned for him all along.

THIS SCAN SHOWS a smaller, changing tumor. A year after Gavin was supposed to die, he walks ahead of me to the car, with a hop in his step. After being in a wheelchair, and being dependent on care for months, he is gaining his independence again, not needing help with things like getting into the car.

"Mom?" Gavin says sweetly while he buckles himself.

"Yeah Gav, what's up?" I reply as we exit the red ramp at Children's Hospital.

"Thank you for believing in me," he says so maturely.

"Of course, Buddy," I reply softly.

WE GET USED to a new normal, a predictable normal, where Gavin needs an ablation procedure every six months or so. He begins a stimulant medicine which helps his mental fatigue. This makes a huge difference once he enters third grade. In a year, he went from a kindergarten reading level to grade two. Slowly, he's catching up. For two and a half years, he mostly stays out of the hospital with the occasional scan or ablation. Gavin continues the Palbociclib until we think the bully is down for good. In June 2015, he stops taking it, and the tumor doesn't grow back.

A YEAR LATER, in June of 2016, we destroy Joe Bully using two laser fibers during one procedure. Gavin is told for now, he is done. After a total of twenty-six surgeries, he gets a reprieve with no treatment planned. In the cancer world, this would be called a remission—a break in treatment where no new cells are being duplicated. In a year, Dr. Petronio will decide if anything more will be done. If needed, he could perform another ablation.

Growing Teratoma Syndrome is curable, only when the tumor can be fully resected. In the brain, when this is not feasible, patients used to die. Now, Gavin and his team of doctors are creating a new protocol. There are clinical trials for pediatric patients for both the Palbociclib, the drug from Pfizer, and for the laser ablation. Gavin is changing the way his disease is treated, as well as many other cancers and diseases such as epilepsy, which the laser also works to eradicate.

If I close my eyes, it's almost like none of this happened. It almost feels like it was a nightmare, as I had hoped in the beginning. The scars and after effects remind us though. They remind us that Gavin—through all he endured—remained strong and brave. His faith pushed all of us. Faith that created miracles.

I believe God brought His light down to Gavin, so we could all see it too.

Gavin (9) being a kid again. June 2015.

Gavin, age 9 in Florida. April 2016.

Be Strong and Brave

Epilogue

What does it mean to be strong and brave? To conquer life's trials and tribulations? For Gavin, it means never giving up and enduring great suffering with the faith that God will be with him wherever he goes. The scars on his body remind us of each surgery and poke. They remind us of the pain. They also tell a story about how faith can create miracles, and that those miracles may not always be quick and easy. In Gavin's case, the miracle was in his endurance and faith, which finally led to his cure.

At the beginning of this journey, I was not strong. I was weak and on my knees begging for God to show up. It was through the darkness, I saw light. There, I gave my worries and fear to God every day, and I followed Gavin's unwavering faith. My motherly instinct to protect Gavin deeply interfered with my faith, until I realized, that God was protecting him all along.

Throughout this journey, many have told me that God only gives you what you can handle. I never knew how to take this because I did not feel like I was handling it. I was drowning and scared, and handling it was my only option. This phrase implies God gave Gavin a brain tumor. I cannot believe a loving God, would do this to His child.

I do think God brings His light down when we are in complete, vast darkness. When we don't know which direction to go, He leads us. Here's the thing though, it is our choice to let that light in and set aside what we think we are capable of in this life without Him. If we are humble and listen, He will illuminate a path.

Gavin's faith saved his life. He would tell me, "Mom, please don't cry, I am going to make it, you just have to believe me."

When we followed Gavin's faith, we created miracles. This is God's message. Not only to a dying boy in a hospital bed, but to all of us. We should not wait for miracles, we should use whatever we have, to push for more. When it looks like there is no hope, we can't give into fear.

Gavin is now ten years old and finishing up fourth grade. He is currently a purple belt in karate and continues to be monitored closely at Children's Hospital of Minnesota. The laser ablation used on Gavin is now being used as first line treatment for difficult to remove tumors such as Gavin's, in place of invasive craniotomies. Children's Hospitals of Minnesota is leading this study, with Dr. Schultz, Dr. Petronio, and Dr. Bendel. Many children will not suffer like Gavin did, because he did.

Gavin's courage to never give up had a ripple effect. It saved him. More than that, it opened trials for many kids and challenged the way standard treatment is viewed for brain tumors. Brain tumor treatment is now more individualized, and more targeted therapies, vaccines, immunotherapies, and minimally invasive techniques, are being used.

Now that Gavin is getting older, I asked him why he wasn't scared when all of the bad things kept happening. He replied instantly, "Well, I wasn't scared because I knew God would give my doctors what they needed." His faith is beyond reason, and is stronger than mine. Gavin has taught me how to live with faith, not fear.

It is because of God's message to Gavin that the impossible became possible. Looking back at what we faced and the miraculous recoveries repeatedly throughout Gavin's illness, I know without faith, he would not be here, alive and well, today.

If you believe, or you don't believe, the message is the same. Be strong, and be brave. Do not go through life in fear, but rather, hope that someday, things will get better. I will leave you with this. It is Gavin's favorite quote from *The Lorax*. One of the many movies he could quote all the way through.

Unless someone like you cares a whole awful lot,
it's not going to get better, it's not.

Dr. Seuss

Acknowledgements

This account of Gavin's journey is my truth as I remember it. I utilized my journaling on Caring Bridge to help reconstruct the events, conversations, and details as accurately as possible. Although I have done much research on Gavin's disease, I am not a doctor, and this manuscript should not be considered medical advice. My opinions formed throughout our journey, are just that. My opinions, which are based on my experiences.

Steve and I are grateful for the wonderful care Gavin has received at Children's Hospitals of St. Paul and Minneapolis in Minnesota. Dr. Petronio, Dr. Schultz, and Dr. Bendel, thank you for fighting with us, for never giving up and listening to our concerns. Without you, Gavin would not be here today. Thank you to the nurses, especially nurse Travis, technicians, therapists, and all staff at Children's for their support over the past four years.

Pfizer, thank you for giving us hope. The moment we knew the medicine was coming, our world of uncertainty changed and we were able to fight again. Thank you for your compassion, and the huge risk you took, as it was our only chance at a future for Gavin. Caring Bridge, thank you for allowing me an outlet to deal with the extreme stress and emotion that came with this fight.

Dr. Lisa Bishop, my aunt, who filled me with faith in God, and who explained in great detail all that I needed to know. Thank you for your support and guidance while we searched for more. Mom and Dad, the love you have instilled in me since I was a little girl, has allowed me to take risks and be what I want to be. Thank you for believing I could and encouraging me every step of the way.

Gavin's followers, who have supported him during this journey, thanks for your encouragement and kindness. My editor Michelle, thanks for believing me and helping me realize things my own eyes couldn't see. Your professionalism and expertise helped me feel confident in my story.

Grace, Gavin, and Gage. You are everything to me. I never knew how much love I could have for another human being until I held each of you in my arms. You fill my days with joy and purpose. Although I selfishly tell you not to grow up, I can't wait to see what you become. When life gets tough, be still, and know that God is with you wherever you go.

Steve—you know, babe. You know my heart more than I do. Life has been tough, but I know we can do it. I am so blessed to call you my husband.

54538536R00151

Made in the USA
Lexington, KY
20 August 2016